SAE EDGE™
RESEARCH REPORT

Unsettled Topics in the Application of Satellite Navigation to Air Traffic Management

James L. Farrell, Ph.D.
VIGIL, Inc.

EDGE DEVELOPMENT TEAM

Dana A. Goward, *Resilient Navigation and Timing Foundation and Maritime Governance, LLC*

Dorota Grejner-Brzezinska, Ph.D., *Ohio State University College of Engineering*

Tim Murphy, *Boeing*

Maj. Ron Ogan, *Civil Air Patrol*

Logan Scott, *Logan Scott Consulting*

Doug Taggart, *Overlook Systems Technologies, Inc.*

Erik Theunissen, Ph.D., *Netherlands Defence Academy*

Maarten Uijt de Haag, Ph.D., *Technische Universität Berlin*

William Woodward, *SAE International Aerospace Avionics Systems Division*

SAE INTERNATIONAL®

Warrendale, Pennsylvania, USA

About the Publisher

SAE International® is a global association of more than 128,000 engineers and related technical experts in the aerospace, automotive and commercial-vehicle industries. Our core competencies are life-long learning and voluntary consensus standards development. Visit sae.org

SAE EDGE™ Research Report Disclaimer

SAE EDGE™ Research Reports focus on topics that are dynamic, in which knowledge is incomplete, and which have yet to be standardized. They represent the collective wisdom of a group of experts and serve as a practical guide to the reader in understanding unsettled subject matter. They are not meant to provide a recommended practice or protocol. The experts have assembled as a community of practitioners to contribute and collectivize their thoughts and points of view; these are not the positions of the institutions or businesses with which they are affiliated, nor is one contributor's perspective advanced over other contributors. SAE EDGE™ Research Reports are the property of SAE International and SAE alone is responsible for their content.

About This Publication

SAE EDGE™ Research Reports provide state-of-the-art and state-of-industry examinations of the most significant topics in mobility engineering. SAE EDGE™ contributors are experts from research, academia, and industry who have come together to explore and define the most critical advancements, challenges, and future direction in areas such as vehicle automation, unmanned aircraft, cybersecurity, advanced propulsion, advanced manufacturing, Internet of Things, and connectivity.

Related Resources

SAE MOBILUS® Automated & Connected Knowledge Hub
https://saemobilus.sae.org/automated-connected

SAE Team

Frank Menchaca, Chief Growth Officer
Michael Thompson, Director, Standards, Information and Research Publications
Monica Nogueira, Acquisitions Director
Beth Ellen Dibeler, Product Manager
William Kucinski, Managing Technical Editor

Printed in USA

EPR2020010
ISSN 2640-3536
e-ISSN 2640-3544
ISBN 978-1-4686-0178-7

To purchase bulk quantities, please contact: SAE Customer Service

E-mail: CustomerService@sae.org
Phone: 877-606-7323 (*inside USA and Canada*)
+1-724-776-4970 (*outside USA*)
Fax: +1-724-776-0790

https://www.sae.org/publications/edge-research-reports

About the Editor

James L. Farrell earned his MS in Engineering from UCLA in 1961 and his Ph.D. in Electrical Engineering from the University of Maryland in 1967. He is an Institute of Navigation (ION) fellow, former ION Air Representative, Life Senior Member of IEEE, former local board member of AIAA, registered professional engineer in Maryland, and member of various scholastic honorary fraternities. His technical experience includes teaching at Marquette University and UCLA, two years each at Minneapolis Honeywell and Bendix Pacific, and 31 years at Westinghouse in design, simulation, and validation of navigation and tracking programs.

Farrell is the author of *Integrated Aircraft Navigation* (Academic Press, 1976; now in paperback after five hard-cover printings); *GNSS Aided Navigation & Tracking: Inertially Augmented Or Autonomous* (2007) – see JamesLFarrell.com – plus chapters in books edited by C.T. Leondes and by Cary Spitzer, and over 100 manuscripts (journal or conference papers, columns in *GPSWorld*, *InsideGNSS*, and *Washington Technology*). His section on satnav/inertial integration will appear in *Position Navigation* & *Timing technologies in the 21st Century*, co-edited by Brad Parkinson, to appear in 2020.

With VIGIL Inc., Farrell served as co-chairman of RTCA's GPS Integrity Working Group. During this time, he continued teaching (at the university-, industry-, and conference-level) and consulting (for private industry, the U.S. Department of Defense, and university research programs).

Most recently, Farrell has focused his efforts on Global Positioning System/inertial integration research, calibration, and integrity – writing programs validated by in-flight data from Ohio University – and three-dimensional geometric morphometrics. However, his scope includes any and all modes of navigation integration (including visual/IMU, increasingly common in recent times).

contents

About the Editor

Unsettled Topics in the Application of Satellite Navigation to Air Traffic Management . . . 3

Introduction . . . 4
State of the Industry . . . 4
Unsettled Topics in the Application of Satellite Navigation to Air Traffic Management . . . 4
Ground Rules . . . 5

Flight Operations . . . 6
NextGen: January 1, 2020 . . . 6
NextGen: "Start-Up Transients" . . . 6
Recommendations . . . 6

Robustness/Resilience . . . 7
Recommendations . . . 8

Data Validation . . . 8
Authentication . . . 8
Integrity . . . 8
Recommendations . . . 8

Data Sharing (Communications) . . . 8
Some Factors Are Less Clear . . . 8
Recommendations . . . 9

Integration and Federation . . . 9
Focus on the Important Information . . . 9
Why Individual Measurements Are So Important . . . 9
Dynamics . . . 10
Recommendations . . . 11

Guidance Strategies . . . 11
This Needs to Be the New Way . . . 11
It Can Be Done . . . 11
Recommendations . . . 12

Man-Machine Interface . . . 13
Not Everything Labeled AI Is Really Artificial . . . 13
This Is One Area Where a "Go Slow" Incremental Approach Can Serve Well . . . 14
Recommendations . . . 14

Administration, Awareness, and Coordination . . . 14
Enough Information? . . . 14
What Did and Did Not Happen . . . 14
Recommendations . . . 14

Summary . . . 14

Appendices . . . 15

Appendix 1: Precise Position Methods and Successes . . . 15

Appendix 2: Integration . . . 15

Appendix 3: Integrity . . . 16

Appendix 4: Role of Other Navaids . . . 16

Appendix 5: Integrity Test ("Spiders in the Woodpile") . . . 16

Appendix 6: Modern Estimation Methods Are Covered . . . 17

Appendix 7: Navigation and Tracking Similarities and Differences . . . 17

Appendix 8: How Much Modeling Error Is Excessive? . . . 18

Appendix 9: Transmitted Measurements with Respect to Center of Gravity . . . 18

Appendix 10: High Accuracy in Velocity without High Accuracy in Position . . . 19

Appendix 11: "Unlikely" Isn't a Strong Enough Condition . . . 20
Ramifications of Inapplicable Gaussian Models . . . 21
Additional Ramifications from Another Direction . . 21

SAE EDGE™ Research Reports . . . 22
Next Steps for the Application of Satellite Navigation to Air Traffic Management . . . 22
Recommendations . . . 22
Definitions . . . 23
Acknowledgements . . . 23
References . . . 24
Contact Information . . . 28

Atosan/Shutterstock.com

Unsettled Topics in the Application of Satellite Navigation to Air Traffic Management

Abstract

Contemporary air traffic management (ATM) challenges are both (1) acute and (2) growing at rates far outpacing established ways for absorbing technological innovation. Lack of timely response will guarantee failure to meet demands. Immediately that creates a necessity to identify means of coping and judging new technologies based on possible speed of adoption. Paralleling the challenges are developments in capability, both recent and decades old. Some steps (e.g., Global Positioning System (GPS) backup) are well known and, in fact, should have progressed further long ago. Others (e.g., sharing raw measurements instead of position fixes) are equally well known and, if followed by further flight tests initiated (and successful) years ago, would have produced a wealth of in-flight experience by now if development had continued. Other possibilities (e.g., automated pilot override) are much less common and are considered largely experimental.

This SAE EDGE™ Research Report is aimed at focusing industry attention on unsettled ATM issues and activities that appear most likely to offer solutions, starting with the near term and continuing on toward increasing versatility and confidence as experience accumulates. In general, the more familiar developments tend to suggest quicker acceptance of test trial initiation, while comparatively unexplored techniques call for a more gradual assimilation. Flexibility for growth is needed in any event, without the pervasive delays that have obstructed progress for so long.

NOTE: SAE EDGE™ Research Reports are intended to identify and illuminate key issues in emerging, but still unsettled, technologies of interest to the mobility industry. The goal of SAE EDGE™ Research Reports is to stimulate discussion and work in the hope of promoting and speeding resolution of identified issues. SAE EDGE™ Research Reports are not intended to resolve the challenges they identify or close any topic to further scrutiny.

JAMES L. FARRELL, PH.D.
VIGIL, Inc.

Edge Development Team

Dana A. Goward, *Resilient Navigation and Timing Foundation and Maritime Governance, LLC*
Dorota Grejner-Brzezinska, Ph.D., *Ohio State University College of Engineering*
Tim Murphy, *Boeing*
Maj. Ron Ogan, *Civil Air Patrol*
Logan Scott, *Logan Scott Consulting*
Doug Taggart, *Overlook Systems Technologies, Inc.*
Erik Theunissen, Ph.D., *Netherlands Defence Academy*
Maarten Uijt de Haag, Ph.D., *Technische Universität Berlin*
William Woodward, *SAE International Aerospace Avionics Systems Division*

ISSN 2640-3536

Introduction

State of the Industry

It has often been observed that, if air traffic management (ATM) were being designed for the first time today, it would differ markedly from its present form. The reason is an ever-present necessity for backward compatibility in the presence of constant challenges - including changing conditions in traffic density, available provisions, and technology. Sweeping changes have been brought by satellite navigation. *Satellite Navigation for Aviation in 2025* [1] offers clear descriptions of satellite systems and signals, usage and performance in aviation with coverage, monitoring - via Receiver Autonomous Integrity Monitoring (RAIM), Satellite Based Augmentation System (SBAS), or Ground Based Augmentation System (GBAS) - having different capabilities for different flight phases and conditions, in the presence of error sources including occasional severe degradation, requiring coordination among those involved in implementing changes in methods or procedures. Historically, backward compatibility has been satisfied by pacing change with balance between old and new systems (e.g., a localizer look-alike approach allows for the usage of customary guidance methods while generating the requisite commands from GPS, thus exploiting advanced capability without surrendering familiarity [2]). Despite admirable accommodation over many decades, continued success is at risk; evolving conditions can outrun managed responsiveness (e.g., sluggish progress and even destruction of provisions [3, 4, 5] useful for urgently needed GPS backup [6]). To avoid being overrun by events, change is essential in procedures, requirements, pacing, and even some key concepts and definitions.

Much requisite change is acknowledged in ongoing deliberations of long-term plans for ATM. For example, Trajectory Based Operations (TBO) discussions envision communications, control, and implementation methodology transitioning in ways not yet clear, with the need for "robust accurate positioning as a given." Reality check: that critical need will not materialize spontaneously from desirous imaginings. The industry has to make it happen, and that's far from given. Even with success in achieving high accuracy (Appendix 1), that notion of positioning is wide of the mark. One main point to be made here is predominance of velocity over instantaneous position accuracy and the indispensable role of integrating shared raw measurements (Appendix 2) to achieve it:

> *"Using raw data to produce the highest possible level of position, velocity, and time accuracy... doing less would leave information on the table and could result in insufficiently precise location and navigation. This would imperil users and the transportation system as a whole."*
>
> **Dana A. Goward, Resilient Navigation and Timing Foundation (RNTF)**

Changes must therefore include some that are fundamental, in ways not practiced by the industry thus far. Only necessary redirection is addressed here; the goal is to augment ATM within a limited scope, not to presumptuously reinvent the enormous body of work already accomplished for it.

A broader perspective can now be expressed in a brief overview. The goal is to obtain safe flight operations (Domain 1) coordinated for both three dimensions (3D) in the air and two dimensions on the ground with robustness (Domain 2). This robustness can come only by rejecting invalid data while retaining valid data (Domain 3) and making the valid information accessible to participants (Domain 4). It must be processed with the best navigation and tracking methods (Domain 5) for generating guidance commands (Domain 6) that take advantage of best-known control techniques including man-machine interactions (Domain 7). All these objectives will require widespread awareness (Domain 8) of people in government, industry, professional institutions, and academia.

Unsettled Topics in the Application of Satellite Navigation to Air Traffic Management

These issues, not exhaustive, were selected for this report of limited length because their difficulty arises from considerations unpursued for various reasons. Some are unsettled because they're relatively recent, some because of changing conditions, others because the industry has not accepted demands they imply. All require change. Breaking ingrained habits will be among the most challenging aspects prescribed here for success. Some brief examples follow:

- Domain 1: Flight operations
- Domain 2: Robustness/Resilience
- Domain 3: Data validation
- Domain 4: Data sharing (communications)
- Domain 5: Integration and federation
- Domain 6: Guidance strategies
- Domain 7: Man-machine interface
- Domain 8: Administration, awareness, and coordination

Historically the Federal Radionavigation Plan (FRP) has defined integrity in terms of a timely warning when a specified error threshold is exceeded. But, as *SATZAP: A Novel Approach to GPS Integrity* [7] noted, if that threshold is tripped only with extreme rarity, even a 50-percent missed detection probability would produce an excellent joint probability of excessive error and failure to promptly detect it. That called into question an official definition for one of the four pillars of Required Navigation Performance (RNP). Then, what about the others?

A continuously maintained path history, regularly updated in a properly designed Extended Kalman Filter (EKF), is widely known (and often used) to withstand short lapses in availability. That circumvents an unnecessarily strict requirement for a full fix plus RAIM with acceptable geometry "on a silver platter every time" (in snapshot operation that discards valuable information; insufficient satellite count equals no update [8]).

By maintaining path history, then, integration facilitates continuity - a benefit that can be maximized as follows: covariance elements and known sensitivities present therein enable probabilistic performance levels to be quantified. "Loss of GPS" can be contingent on variances and adherence of measurement residuals to their corresponding statistics (Appendix 3).

Even more obvious is the dramatic improvement in another RNP criterion: accuracy. In marked contrast to treating coordinates as if they were measurements (they're NOT), integration maximizes effectiveness of all information and accounts for known sensitivities. That dramatic improvement is "sine qua non," or essential for providing velocity information adequate for collision avoidance (CA). Unsettled topic sections substantiate statements made here. Absence of requisite improvements, then, leaves current methods unable to satisfy future ATM needs in heavy air traffic. Revisiting of RNP performance is thus inescapable.

Discussion to follow compares future vs present practices, the latest being Automatic Dependent Surveillance - Broadcast (ADS-B) OUT/IN modes, for which assessments vary widely from

- Upbeat promises of net-centric operations, performance-based service, weather assimilated into decision making, adaptive security, Positioning, Navigation, and Timing (PNT) services, TBO, equivalent visual operations, and high-density arrival/departure [9]

  to

- Lower-than-expected performance in most or all of those features (painfully clear in some cases from publication titles, e.g., [10,11]), which naturally raises the question "Who is right?"

Rather than taking sides, it is prudent to highlight a central fact: The Federal Aviation Administration (FAA) prohibits acting on ADS-B data unless verified by information independent of satellite navigation. Lack of security is the reason given, but velocity inaccuracy alone severely limits ADS-B. At any rate, closer spacing between planes incurs risk that grows progressively with increases in air traffic.

Closer spacing is dangerous even at present. Accounts of near-miss events, even from sources not recognized as authoritative, cannot be easily dismissed. Growth of those events with growing traffic is inescapable unless inevitable closer spacing is accommodated by dramatically better accuracy. The need to project, well in advance, RELATIVE distances at CLOSEST APPROACH TIMES lay dormant throughout almost the entire industry for years. Delay in facing problems is readily traceable to "accentuate-the-positive" traditions, common in business and institutions today as noted in the *Beukers January 2001 keynote address* [12]. Abandoning "business as usual" habits thus appears fittingly among decisions governing material herein, cited next.

Ground Rules

- Focus is on nonmilitary operation with most passenger aircraft not maneuvering most of the time, but with recognition of rules needed to cover exceptions.
- Safety demands a new requirement for cybersecurity in all communications involved. [13]
- Processing capability is huge but finite. Critical functions must be faithfully executed in a straightforward fashion that avoids undue complexity.
- Legal issues, easily enough to warrant a separate study, appear only in limited ways where warranted within specific discussions.
- Primary attention is given to operation wherein Global Navigation Satellite System (GNSS) signals are present most of the time and any inauthentic signals are extracted, with backup providing lower performance otherwise assuming control (Appendix 4).
- Much progress has been made in *Alternative Positioning, Navigation, and Timing (APNT)* [14], characterized here as integrated within other unsettled issues. It will not be long, however, before increased traffic will further increase its importance, justifying further development. Many considerations raised herein will then apply with different parameters.
- The possibility of today's GNSS becoming unusable from overwhelming interference is neither denied nor analyzed in depth. Conceivable alternatives include a medley of Low Earth Orbiters (LEOs), producing stronger signals from closer proximity and with ephemeris provisions via heavier orbit computations and/or intersatellite links [15]. Pseudo-satellites (or "pseudolites"), without the ephemeris, but with added receiver dynamic range issues, could be another substitute. With adjustments, then, operation with direct measurements can otherwise be largely as described; principles herein remain applicable.
- Nothing needed for safety can be proprietary. Safety has top priority.

The overriding importance of safety necessitates addressing how it can be compromised. Vigilance is needed to prevent ill-advised administrative decisions (e.g., Loran shutdown) and to discourage various common profit-oriented business practices (e.g., proprietary software plus other profit-enhancement-to-the-detriment-of-value expedients, and - finally - just plain complacency).

Just as success demands facing hard realities, it also encourages taking advantage of capabilities not sufficiently exploited. The enormous benefit offered by sharing individual measurements is one example. As another, many operations have a need for information frequently expressed in terms of a choice ("either/or"). Today's processing capabilities accommodate both, in tandem; the presence of one does not preclude the presence of other (Appendix 2 notes multiple combinations of federated and integrated solutions furnished concurrently). A similar advantage can be exploited with a concurrent absolute and relative nav (or "relnav") grid with each participant having its own separate absolute nav errors that don't affect relative perceptions. Still another example is the release from the unnecessary limitations of loose coupling. [16]

Flight Operations

NextGen: January 1, 2020 [17]

From the beginning of 2020, all aircraft required to be equipped with transponders must transmit at least

- Once per second while airborne or while moving on the airport surface

  and

- Once every five seconds while stationary on the airport surface

ADS-B output messages via either

- Mode S extended squitter (ES)

  or

- Universal Access Transceiver (UAT), with different limits on allowable latency (total, uncompensated, and negative)

Immediately it is noted here that latency effects can be substantially mitigated via track file maintenance. When velocity does not change much during that interval, for example, instead of

$$\text{velocity} \times \text{latency}$$

the effect is reduced to essentially

$$\text{error in estimated velocity} \times \text{latency} + \text{velocity} \times \text{uncertainty in latency}$$

NextGen: "Start-Up Transients"

Examples include [18,19]:

- Installation errors (200 cases per month): Of the 27,000 ADS-B Out installations, about 5,000 - over 80 percent of those being single-engine general aviation (GA) aircraft - have performance problems or transmit incorrect data, e.g., a wrong International Civil Aviation Organization (ICAO) code, incorrect flight identification, or Dual-Out boxes with different ICAO codes (the latter can arise from equipping an aircraft with both UAT and ES)
- Reception of Flight Information Services - Broadcast (FIS-B) and Traffic Information Services - Broadcast (TIS-B) may be dependent on altitude and/or location
- GA aircraft may not be compliant with the requirement for either ES or UAT output
- Mode-S transponders might exceed the two-second latency maximum in some weather conditions
- Mode-S transponder ICAO codes may be incorrect or broadcast as duplicate codes
- Small Unmanned Aircraft Systems (sUAS) have interfered with manned aircraft flights and airport activities. Although larger Unmanned Aircraft Systems (UAS) are being inspected to manned aircraft requirements, that is not true of those weighing less than 55 pounds.

Additional examples [20] include missing barometric pressure altitude, invalid Mode 3/A Code, incorrect emitter category, and aircraft position errors. There are additional compliance issues, not only for GA aircraft but also for airports providing NextGen-compliant equipment. No claim of thoroughness is implied here; a complete portrayal would require a longer and more focused document.

Recommendations

All recommendations - except the last item - are aimed at improving safety:

- Require that all avionics installation be tested against FAA requirements before aircraft inspections are completed. Add re-verification to aircraft annual inspections.
- Resolve issues for sUAS flights at night and in Beyond Visual Line Of Sight (BVLOS) operation. Choices can err on the side of safety, facilitated by a return-to-base option, relatively painless for UAS.
- Determine the effects of weather on ADS-B latency requirements and publish guidance - and always exploit the means to mitigate latency effects as described above.

- Begin offering electronic charts through FAA flight service station (FSS).
- Require visual flight rule (VFR) flight plans beginning or ending in controlled airspace.
- Expand Federal Acquisition Regulation (FAR) 14 Code of Federal Regulations (CFR) Part 107 to develop airspace requirements for all UAS. [21]
- Develop or specify maintenance requirements for sUAS and UAS for flight safety including operation over people and critical infrastructure.
- Follow FAA's recently released UAS Safety Risk Management Policy [22, 23, 24] offering draft plans for establishing a safe and affordable set of services (U-space) providing digitized automated functions and procedures, with risk assessment, for efficient and secure UAS Traffic Management (UTM).
- Follow the proposed rule [25, 26] requiring UAS in flight to provide remote identification and tracking information for certain recipients (on ground and other airspace users) in the National Airspace System (NAS). Coordinating manned and unmanned traffic will affect both communication and integration; see unsettled Domains 4 and 5 for further ramifications.
- To reduce execution costs, initially relax NextGen ADS-B compliance in Class A, B, and C airspace.

Robustness/Resilience

Flight operations in U.S.-controlled airspace obviously necessitate presence of supporting inputs plus backups to survive in their absence. Self-evident as that may seem, progress on securing both halves has suffered. Jamming and spoofing (Figure 1) have taxed countermeasures (e.g., as described in [27, 28, 29, 30, 31, 32]), while backup, though long recognized

FIGURE 1. **Spoofing attacks.**

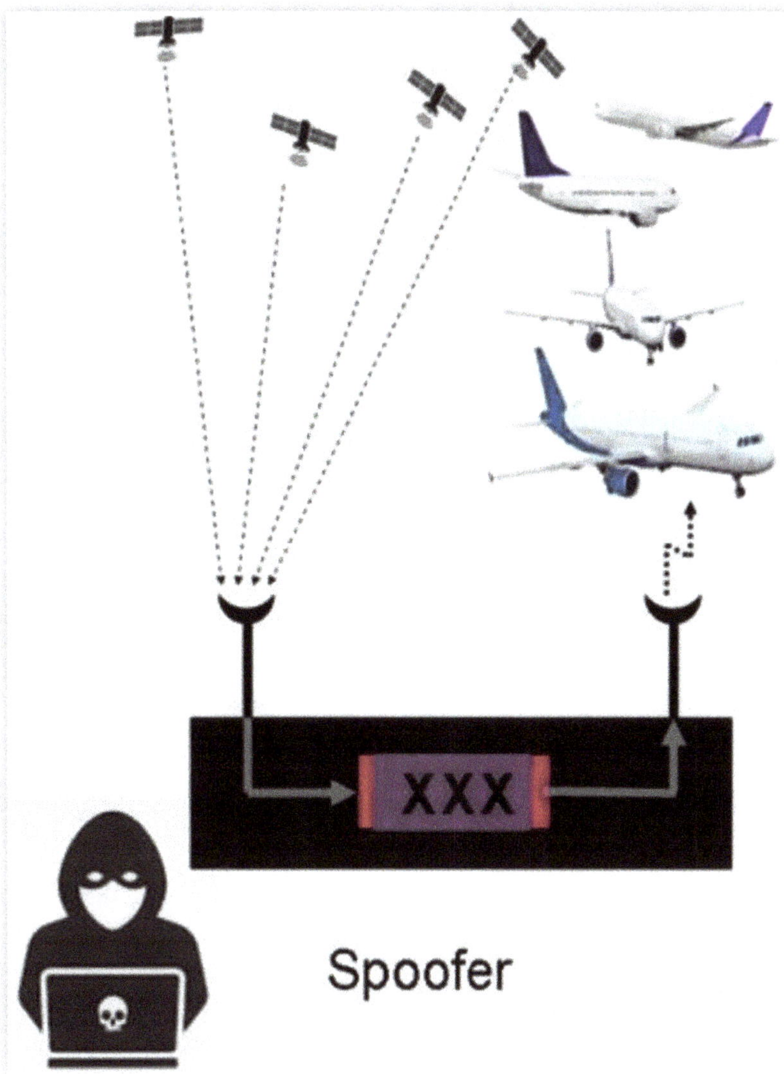

Le_Mon/Shutterstock.com; Ewa Studio/Shutterstock.com; A-spring/Shutterstock.com

as urgent [6,33], got off to a slow start as transmitting towers for Loran, an independent backup means [3, 4, 5], were largely dismantled. The RNTF has been urging decision-makers to take action. While advocacy continues, the response is unaccountably slow.

Recommendations

It goes without saying: no robustness = no mission success; robustness/resilience is essential. Expedite programs to detect and overcome attacks, continue ongoing development for backup via APNT means, and be prepared to make the most of whatever valid data can be accessed. Heed the urgings just mentioned from RNTF that cite repeated spoofing at sea attacks, and interpret those maritime experiences as a grave warning for aviation.

Data Validation

Hand in hand with robust operation is the obvious need to validate incoming data. That task includes two broad categories, (1) verifying received signal sources as GNSS satellites, not spoofed (authentication) and (2) disallowing any GNSS measurements which though authentic are nevertheless erroneous (integrity). Both tasks, involving substantial complexity, have fortunately experienced considerable progress.

Authentication

European Union (EU) documentation [34], with STRIKE3 [35] and references cited therein, show and share considerable work towards analyzing interference, threat reporting, and standards [36] for receiver test. With meaconing/spoofing and jamming addressed, STRIKE3 provides criteria to evaluate various receiver designs. One protective design approach with particular strength, named Chimera [37], uses encryption keys and withholds authentication until after opportunities for meaconing attacks have largely elapsed. Several years after its development, that vital feature is finally being prepared for use; follow-through is in progress.

In-depth description of various protective approaches is offered in *Improving the Operation and Development of Global Positioning System (GPS) Equipment Used by Critical Infrastructure* [38]; developments executed and continuing through recent years are reported in *Toughening GPS Receivers Against Interference: Ensuring Signal Reception in Spectrally Busy Environments* [39] and *Anti-Jamming for Airborne Platforms* [40].

Integrity

Even signals correctly recognized as authentic may be unacceptable due to a control segment flaw [41], excess propagation effects (iono, tropo, multipath), or receiver defects. Though much has been accomplished toward establishing integrity, follow-through has been poor (Appendix 5).

Recommendations

All facets of development just cited deserve cooperation and all integrity test flaws noted in Appendix 5 need to be corrected. Increased future usage of integration will enlarge the benefits of separate integrity checks discussed in Appendix 3. Above all, encrypt. [13]

Data Sharing (Communications)

With many choices made regarding NextGen data link capacity, modes of modulation, synchronization, bandwidth, power, etc. - one item stands out. The ubiquitous interrogation/response of yesteryear is fundamentally inadequate; one participant's signal is every other participant's interference. The cacophony of synchronous garble during Desert Storm, for example, rendered communications practically useless. [42] Instead of that in crowded airspace, a vast improvement is for each participant - moving or stationary - to have an assigned time slot to transmit once during every full transmit cycle as in ADS-B. Every participant, silent except for that brief interval, can then listen and thereby track every other participant. The hardware, firmware, message size, formats, etc. can match NextGen but one major departure is needed: message information content. Message preamble/synchronization, identification, error detection/correction, etc. can take whatever form is appropriate but, for all of the reasons shown in the next unsettled domain, raw measurements rather than coordinates need to be shared. [43, 44, 45] That course of action has already been validated in flight. [46] A further addition: objects to avoid must obviously include those sending signals and those that don't (rogue non-participants). Tracks for the latter can be enabled by shared line of sight message types (pp. 203-204 of [47]) or other means.

Some Factors Are Less Clear

The Federal Communications Commission (FCC) spectrum allocation might not be compatible with FAA safety requirements. Examples include unregulated frequency bands used by sUAS, and UAT/1090ES incompatibility with incoming international aircraft. Decisions have not yet been made for two other key items: authority (e.g., in air or on the ground) and capacity. The in-air versus on-ground decision will await the choice made for control authority (next to last unsettled issue addressed in this report). For the latter item, capacity will be a small fraction of a saturation number:

$$(\text{area covered by COMM system})/$$
$$(\text{square of minimum separation distance})$$

multiplied by the number of flight levels (e.g., two to three dozen; varying among regions). How small that fraction will have to be depends on how far from gridlock the system must always remain, and also on compromises inevitably required involving data rates. High traffic density in some regions can involve hundreds of participants. ES length of 112 microseconds can allow hundreds of time-shared messages to be transmitted every second, so every participant could receive a message from every other participant at 1 Hz. But with randomized transmit times, various departures from ideal conditions, encryption, etc., extant data link parameters will be insufficient for ubiquitous updating every second.

Furthermore, update rates above 1 Hz can be desired for tracking during maneuvers (which temporarily increase errors via lags and transients in EKF trackers). Also, message types other than updates (e.g., intent [48]) are always needed. For those reasons this integrated design concept must be "Post-NextGen," unshackled from existing plans. Though stated judiciously, more bandwidth will be required. Parameters cannot of course be firmly established here, but a few points can moderate the demand - measurements are needed, but not from every Space Vehicle (SV) every time if cyclic selection can be allowed. Also, more than one carrier phase value can fit in an ES message, since only changes over one second are needed.

UAS communication needs are not defined. Contemplating local networks or long-term evolution (LTE) for that will leave security (therefore safety) unsubstantiated. Relaying UAS position reports would produce the same weakness (crude velocity producing defective projection to closest approach) already cited as a major limitation of ATM in general (next section).

Recommendations

Decisions to be made will involve ever-present tradeoffs between performance, complexity, cost, spectrum, etc. As always, design will need to be balanced between conflicting objectives.

Integration and Federation

Having accurate satellite navigation data is necessary but, alone, it is not enough to achieve safe operation in congested airspace. Discussion below adds the following conditions:

- Measurements, not coordinates
- The right combination of measurements (pseudoranges and incremental carrier phases)
- Phase information usage to infer dynamics

Recommended changes in established procedures are supported by extensive background and experience (Appendices 6, 7, 8, 9) plus results (Appendix 10) about to be described.

Focus on the Important Information

Since the dawn of aviation, air surveillance has been defined in terms of location sequences. That can work over oceans (if frequently updated) but, over increasingly crowded airspace, elementary reasoning exposes a fatal flaw. Consider a pair of position fixes, one with perfect longitude but a kilometer of error in the north direction, and the other with exact latitude but with an east/west position off by a kilometer. Averaging them gives "only" 500 meters of error in both! [45] Position reports treat their error volumes as if they were spherical - though actual shape may conjure up anything from Figure 2b (cigar) to Figure 2a (pancake, or otherwise a "potato pancake" with one intermediate axis of size in between the smallest and the largest) - while wide variations in directional accuracies are ruinously disregarded. By ignoring known correlations and sensitivity variations, position reporting lacks the crucial feature that made Differential Global Positioning System (DGPS) operation spectacularly successful: processing of individual measurements.

Combining individual measurements is nothing new. Ancient mariners, lacking modern luxuries, had no other choice; they had to be resourceful. Centuries later, digitization plus optimal estimation methods led to algorithmic advances offering huge improvements in all phases of navigation and tracking. When those developments began, their easily obtainable benefits were envisioned to become standard practice: [49]

> *"[...] all nav estimates will always account for all data [...] every [...] function [...] will therefore benefit from all that data [...]" "[...] sacrifices [...] will presumably be corrected [...] assimilation of advanced methods into operational systems [...]"*

and shortly after, with growing visibility of satellite navigation, the practice was likewise recommended for phase difference measurements [50]. Unfortunately, acceptance for ATM was glacially slow, but can no longer be delayed.

Why Individual Measurements Are So Important

If imperfections in observations from any SV produce a 10-meter error in my receiver, essentially the same error will affect that SV's measurement seen in other receivers within miles of me. When I subtract my receiver's measurement from another for that SV, then, the 10-meter error will cancel. That rejection of big errors - the essence of differential operation - explains the spectacular success of DGPS. However, it does not happen when I compare my coordinates to yours; our receivers may not be selecting the same SVs. That starts a

FIGURE 2. **Position report error volumes.**

long list of benefits offered by individual measurements (and not by position reports):

- Usage of partial fixes when there aren't enough satellite signals to form a coordinate solution
- Capability to validate integrity (Appendix 3)
- No danger from datum mismatch (scalar measurements are independent of reference frame)
- Allowance of measurement error variations (thereby enabling optimal multisensor operation)
- Ability to account for nonuniform directional sensitivities
- Ability to account for EKF error state correlations
- Further error cancellation, even more beneficial for carrier phase increments over one second

Those one-second increments provide crucial precise velocity accuracy with no catastrophic error, plus extensive additional benefits (Appendix 10) flight-verified in both navigation [47] and tracking. [46]

Despite these compelling features and decades of continued advocacy [43, 51] applicable to growing numbers of operations (now including UASs), directly sharing measurements did not become an adopted standard. Fortunately, the National Space-Based PNT Advisory Board has been gratifyingly supportive of this advocacy; much detail is offered for those interested in [51, 52, 53].

Dynamics

Immediately upon recognition of the error cancellation enabled by subtracting measurements, attention is drawn to what position needs to be accurate: not instantaneous, but the future position - and not just absolute, but relative to all objects that present a potential collision risk. That stems from a reality, again elementary: there is no safety without separation and there is no dependable separation without knowledge of that future position at time of closest approach (TCA). That places the spotlight here on dynamics.

Another instructive example, based solely on arithmetic: Compare two systems - one has initial position accuracy at one centimeter, the other one meter. Both have velocity error of 10 meters per second (a number found in some ADS-B descriptions). Projected ahead, even only a few seconds, is the first appreciably better? No. Next, compare effects of initial velocity errors at one centimeter per second versus 10 meters per second, projected ahead to closest approach time of 100 seconds (a round figure almost enough to give a one kilometer minimum separation from roughly 10 percent speed change in many scenarios [54]):

10 meters/sec × 100 sec = 1000 meter projected uncertainty;
in both horizontal directions:
1000 × 1000 = 1 million square meters

1 cm/sec × 100 sec = 1 meter of uncertainty projected ahead;
in both horizontal directions:
1 × 1 = 1 square meter uncertainty area

Obviously then, the objective must be to form dependably accurate estimates for velocity vectors relative to all objects presenting a risk of collision. Those estimates must be obtained far enough in advance of TCA to initiate horizontal velocity change by gentle maneuvers, with subsequent repetitive trim adequate to maintain sufficient minimum separation. Neither conventional ATM nor NextGen satisfies that requirement, relying instead on the Traffic Collision Avoidance System (TCAS). Abrupt (to passengers, terrifying) climb/dives cannot become an acceptable common occurrence.

Recommendations

The American National Standards Institute (ANSI) Unmanned Aircraft Systems Standardization Collaborative (UASSC) for safe UAS integration into the NAS involves a long list of organizations. [55] The first International Organization for Standardization (ISO) safety standard for UAS was very recently approved. [56] For both manned and unmanned aircraft, adoption of SAE International's satnav receiver standard [53] will enable extension of differential operation beyond requirements for a ground reference, to form track files providing dynamics (velocity and higher-order), giving time histories of 3-D relative motion essential for enabling guidance commands to achieve required separation. Appendix 4 applies that principle to the full set of available sensors. The approach [57] allows a huge benefit in accuracy plus also data editing for integrity, intrinsic backup capability, etc. (i.e., all of the robustness features enumerated earlier). Finally, risk analyses must be based on statistics accounting for "fat-tail" distributions (Appendix 11).

Guidance Strategies

This Needs to Be the New Way

Apart from important considerations of path optimization described elsewhere [58], concentration here is focused on CA. With separation described as either an alternate characterization of that or a precondition for safety, the question arises: Separation from what? The answer, of course, is from everything, whether

- Terrain - the continuum below plus guy wires, dodged by using extant clearance methods
- Other airborne objects
- Ground vehicles or other aircraft on taxiways (to reduce yearly runway incursions, trending generally upward and currently approaching 2000)

...any moving or stationary object to be encountered at any time from departure to destination gate arrival. To maximize safety then, each participant in a scenario must, throughout its journey, repetitively update its closest approach time and minimum projected distance from every other object along its path. If there are hundreds of them then hundreds of track filters must be continuously maintained and, for the subset of potential conflicts (objects with closing range rate), closest approach projections must be repetitively computed. Otherwise there is no basis for confident guidance and collision risk is left unquantified, with danger growing progressively as traffic density increases.

It Can Be Done

The good news is that valid satellite navigation data, properly used, enables the capability just described. Track filters - whether maintained by radar, satnav, or optical measurements - perform as expected with linearization (EKF) in a stable reference frame [59, 60] and today's processing can easily accommodate hundreds of track files at data rates sufficient for model fidelity of path characterization used in each EKF. For nonmaneuvering aircraft, projecting ahead to closest approach (e.g., see Figure 3) is a straightforward vector extrapolation using EKF states and extraction of projected cross track relative position components. That can be followed by repetitive velocity adjustments via speed-up or slow-down commands [54] which, except for conflicts at narrow aspect, produce adequate separation without severe last-moment jerk (Appendix 7). The stipulations - valid and properly used - were covered in unsettled domains 3 and 5, while 4 identified conditions for providing data volumes sufficient to produce update rates demanded by designated capacity requirements. This isn't, then, idle musings of a perfectionist; participants' receivers see signals from the same satellites and, once processed, the results allow determination of closest approach time and separation. The stated goal - each repetitively updating how to avoid all others - incurs the least possible risk.

Guiding away from closest approach with insufficient crossing velocity or for maneuvering aircraft is, unsurprisingly, more challenging. Unlike the simple trim computations just described, a more involved evasion strategy will be required - which can grow to a sequence of maneuvers when crowded airspace presents multiple conflicts concurrently. That subject could easily spawn a separate study in

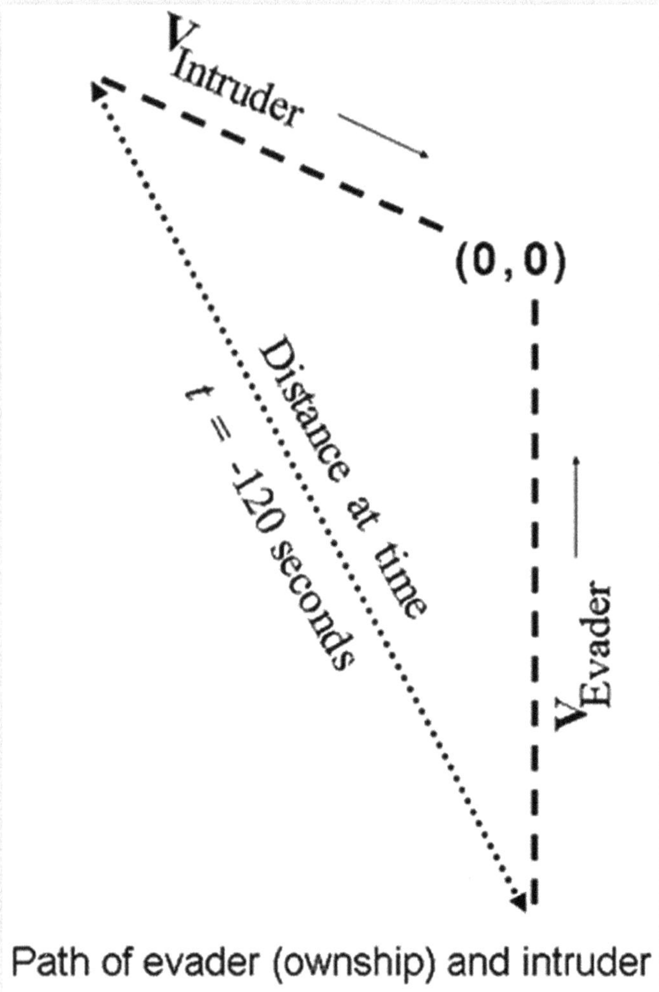

FIGURE 3. For nonmaneuvering aircraft, projecting ahead to closest approach is a straightforward vector extrapolation using EKF states and extraction of projected cross track relative position components.

itself; for immediate purposes here, it suffices to cite existing capabilities. The industry already has people experienced in deciding who moves when, who goes which way, rules of the road, etc. Those familiar with the Airborne Collision Avoidance System (ACAS) [61] or with TCAS III Traffic Alerts (TA) and Resolution Advisories (RA) were able to devise evasive commands (e.g., right turns for both aircraft in potential conflict) from limited information. Pilots and ATM analysts would likely be gratified to have highly accurate 3D velocity vectors; no doubt they could do impressive work with that plus intent information [48] conveyed by additional data link messages. That by no means implies ease of that task, especially with added challenges of the type described in "Lessons Learned: The Rise and Fall of the SESAR ATM improvement program." [62] Nor can we predict choices to emerge from the short-term, long-term, and intermediate duration conflict resolution strategies surveyed in *Conflict Detection and Resolution for Civil Aviation: A Literature Survey* [63] - but appreciable progress has been made [64, 65, 66] and, in any case, dynamic accuracies improved by orders of magnitude will be vital.

Recommendations

Rigorous track processing is essential for confident thorough separation in crowded airspace. Methods, already documented with validation by in-flight data for both navigation [47] and tracking [46], have no proprietary strings. Prompt acceptance combined with evasion studies just mentioned with inclusion of intent [63] message information would expedite preparation for use in operation. In addition to evasion strategies, developments would include carefully and judiciously prescribing bandwidth increase with tradeoffs analyzing data rates versus miss distance. Current plans don't include multitarget track file processing as described herein because, though computation is cheap, spectrum isn't. Still, with streaming entertainment on demand considered affordable, the goal is not out of reach. Start today or wait for tomorrow's traffic to inundate - and don't wait for an emergency before considering questions of liability (Appendix 11).

Man-Machine Interface

The issue of control - who (or what) is in charge - is loaded with controversy. Evidence abounds showing Artificial Intelligence (AI) vastly outperforming humans in tasks involving highly complex and subtle reasoning. Arguments countering those narrations (e.g., the training data can be biased, trusting safety-of-life decisions with anything that can't be explained, whose life is it anyway?, etc.) are likewise familiar and, without attempting to confirm either side, only a few observations are offered. Reluctance of many pilots to surrender control to automation was reinforced by recent experience (i.e., 737 MAX), but a counterargument is offered by success in the military realm.

Not Everything Labeled AI Is Really Artificial

In the Automatic Ground Collision Avoidance System (AGCAS), lifesaving commands were generated via automation rather than human action. Execution of those controls originated from detailed and thorough understanding of an imminent danger and of the environment, based on laws of physics. Following the basic example of Figure 4, required climb initiation time is determined from pullup g-level and responsiveness to commands. That can often demand reflexes beyond capability of a human under pressure. The Automatic Ground Collision Avoidance System (Auto GCAS) video [67] produced by the Air Force Research Laboratory credits AGCAS with saving several pilots. A related development not yet fielded, Automatic Air Collision Avoidance System (AACAS) [68], offers similar potential. For both AGCAS (terrain) and AACAS (other aircraft) - pilot override capability is available. In addition, there are ACAS variants in different forms for different applications that are not automated [61]; their full operation depends upon both intercepting aircraft to be ACAS equipped. [69]

Systems based on physical laws are sometimes loosely characterized as AI. The impression is not only misleading but can impede acceptance of vital safety enhancements. Common resistance to AI in life-or-death decisions has roots not fully applicable to automation based on rigorous analytical design.

FIGURE 4. **Required climb initiation time is determined from pullup g-level and responsiveness to commands.**

VanderWolf Images/Shutterstock.com

This Is One Area Where a "Go Slow" Incremental Approach Can Serve Well

ATM has historically proceeded with a step-by-step response to innovation. It seems likely that adoption of any automatic pilot override condition would at least begin with restriction to explainable (i.e., rigorous physics-based) emergency controls. Further speculation here about transfer of military experience to commercial aviation, or (especially) expanding the scope beyond would be premature. AI and machine learning can reduce pilot cockpit overload but keeping man-in-the-loop is safety critical since automation equipment may fail, requiring manual intervention. In an emergency, the pilot can override regulations.

Recommendations

Absorbing the lessons learned from Air Force experience can be a high-priority step toward defining benefits offered by automatic control to enhance safety under emergency conditions. Recognize the basic difference between analytical versus artificially derived commands. Phasing in of further developments involving AI should begin with gradual measured steps. Especially now with trends toward automating even the training data, prudence is very much in order. Guard against the inclination toward a "vacation from thinking" (exhibited, for example, by continued popularity of loose coupling in our industry).

"Leaving it all to the black box" is clearly hazardous.

Administration, Awareness, and Coordination

Enough Information?

References already cited include tracts from GPS World and InsideGNSS, which have involved ATM among a wide range of applications comprising satellite plus other means of navigation. Within academia there have also been strong meetings containing presentations highly relevant to ATM (e.g., [70]) as well as the flight validations conducted by Ohio University already cited herein (plus well-known contributions, too numerous to list, from other universities). For decades, publications from the Institute of Navigation (IoN) have contributed mightily to the existing store of knowledge and additional professional societies (e.g., SAE International, the Institute of Electrical and Electronics Engineers (IEEE), RNTF, ASTM, RTCA, and others) likewise contributed heavily. Existence of all this information raises an awkward question as to why so much has remained unsettled.

What Did and Did Not Happen

It is first acknowledged that decisions affecting current configurations were made at a time with lower levels of both traffic and interference. Still, though, there were warnings; as the *Beukers January 2001 keynote address* [12] stated, we were on notice, but we didn't notice. That January 2001 keynote cited a prerelease of the *Volpe report* [6], pointing out not only its excellence but also its thoroughness; both should be required reading for decision makers. Many further warnings followed (e.g., [13, 71]). Elements within governments have lately acted on awareness (e.g., [72]).

Another development now decades old is the spectacular success of differential operation which, through exploitation of individual measurements, enabled well-known revolutionary improvements in multiple applications. While those applications used ground stations, advocacy for extension to operation without any stationary reference is now also decades old. [43] With all participants moving, all positions and velocities are relative - just as required for CA! Straightforward adaptation for moving-to-moving scenarios, producing precise velocity history validated in flight, [46] offers vital untapped CA capability.

Recommendations

The most thorough and promising approaches will be ineffective without widespread dissemination (getting the word out) and acceptance (getting the concepts adopted). The latter has been the more challenging. In particular, sharing of raw measurements is resisted by many suppliers (it "interferes with their business model"). Without that feature, though, users are denied differential operation and ability to integrate with other subsystems or perform their own integrity monitoring. Steering that priority toward the direction of safety is the goal of Woodward's "Proposed Guidelines For Resilient PNT Receivers" [53]. Beyond that, administrators lack sufficient time to absorb enough of the right information from the flood of literature plus ubiquitous tutorials and seminars, all with a broad range of quality. Preventing severe future shortcomings will inescapably demand solving that paradox of deficit-despite-overload. Keep getting the word out and find ways to get it accepted.

Summary

The message conveyed by this SAE EDGE™ Research Report follows from the meaning of ATM. Air traffic will continue to experience dramatic changes:

- Flight operations must accommodate far higher traffic density including UASs (Domain 1)
- Operation in the presence of severe interference does, and will continue to, tax resilience (Domain 2)

- Received data will contain increasing amounts of invalid information (Domain 3)
- Existing methods for data sharing have glaring inadequacies (Domain 4)

Therefore, ATM must undergo equally extensive changes:

- Both integrated and federated solutions, not provided by established practice, need to be made available (Domain 5)
- Guidance techniques must capitalize on those marked improvements (Domain 6)
- Control authority must resolve man-machine interaction to execute guidance (Domain 7)
- Cooperation is needed from government, industry, academia, and professional institutions (Domain 8)

Much progress toward these goals has already been achieved. The domain descriptions and appendices contained herein offer answers that are known but need wider dissemination and understanding - plus acceptance. Likewise needed are further steps awaiting decisions not yet made (e.g., ultimate communication system parameters, assignment of authority for control decisions). With challenges growing rapidly, safety will demand adaptation at a pace much faster than anything witnessed thus far.

Additional areas of importance not covered herein are included elsewhere. *Next Generation ATM Systems: Increasing Safety, Efficiency and Sustainability of the Aviation Sector* [73], for example, addresses vehicle health and environmental sustainability plus demand/capacity rebalancing by redirecting multiple aircraft through tactical intervention for unscheduled traffic, departure delays, and variations (seasonal, weekly, hourly, or unforeseen) in wind or weather. Also there are mechanization issues not scrutinized here - for the pilot (text messaging/map/chart/plate/flight bag) or for the controller, plus other items addressed in sources already cited. Rather than being all-inclusive this report highlights essential factors missing from today's ATM and in some cases from present plans, requiring support to ensure their presence in the future.

Appendices

To many readers, the sections that follow will be familiar (even self-evident), but their presence here is justified by (1) a need for wider appreciation, (2) absence of their application in much common operation, and (3) a need to facilitate easy reading of report material unimpeded by constant digression. Every effort is made to express each item succinctly, with prompt recognition and clarity valued above detailed precision and thoroughness. Issues being addressed can be skimmed or omitted by those familiar.

Appendix 1: Precise Position Methods and Successes [74, 75, 76, 77]

Two methods offering high position accuracy are Precise Point Positioning (PPP) and Real Time Kinematic (RTK) positioning, with enhancements and variations that have been added to each. To circumvent hours-long convergence times, for example, PPP used multiple carrier frequencies with multiple constellations. Constrained RTK operation (e.g., which restricted rover distance from base station) was circumvented by having a regional network of stations. Expansion of the network, in fact, produces precision in GNSS navigation messages (clock and ephemeris), paving the way for PPP. Further steps, adding a layer of code (pseudorange) and carrier-phase bias corrections, enabled PPP with ambiguity resolution (PPP-AR). If in addition precise atmospheric information (zenith tropospheric and slant ionospheric delays) is provided to PPP users, then centimeter-level accuracy can be promptly obtained. This unification of the two methods, appropriately, gave way to the name "PPP-RTK." [78]

Appendix 2: Integration

We've known how to do this, even in optimized ways, for over six decades. The opportunity extends to surveillance as well as navigation data, and to combinations of both types. That latter prospect has prompted concerns over causing a single point of failure. That happens if the only output is one obtained from integrating all data. However, integration can be conducted simultaneously at multiple levels and also in tandem with federation. With all data available centrally, every conceivable combination of input data could be independently formed, each including or excluding any source(s) desired. Cross checks and comparisons can then select preferred combinations. In all cases a key feature is usage of measurements, not positions. A statement from *Robust Design for GNSS Integration* [79] was repeated at the end of a 2015 presentation to the National Advisory Board [52]:

> *"The best humanly possible strategy is to deliver whatever performance is reachable from all available information, incomplete as it may be. For decades it has been feasible to combine intermittent partial data - of different types at varying accuracies with different sensitivities from different directions at different times - and extract all benefits offered."*

Practices advocated herein would offer no more and no less than that.

Appendix 3: Integrity

The uninitiated might balk at a task of navigating with a set of measurements including some that might be wrong. Fortunately, the objective is achievable via consistency checks; for GPS that requires more satellite measurements than necessary (e.g., more than four in 3D space with no atomic clock) for a position solution. The classic approach works reliably for detection but, if not expanded beyond to identify or at least exclude faulty data, rejecting the solution brings "guilt by association" (rejecting the good measurements along with the bad).

Volumes have been written about minimizing the loss/risk/damage through various means. Practically all of those well-devised methods are highly sophisticated - far beyond what can be covered here. Ironically, however, one of those schemes paved the way toward the simplest technique conceivable. Covariance elements were used to supplement marginal amounts of measured data. [80] Every complex attribute of that approach fell away when carried to the limit (one individual measurement). Each residual can be tested via single measurement RAIM [81] - divide its absolute value by its theoretical or conservatively computed RMS. Unlike most approaches, the method is applicable to measurements with unequal variances - therefore to any sensor - and can readily reject multiple flawed measurements. Also, pre-whitening enables usage with correlation between measurement errors (pages 71 and 72 of [47]).

Appendix 4: Role of Other Navaids

The crucial importance of GPS and slowness of progress toward mitigating its vulnerability [6] by backup development are thoroughly familiar, needing no further repetition here. Instead, discussion here will focus on progress. As GPS offers both navigation and timing capability, backup is needed for both. One means for backup, (e)Loran, lost most of its available provisions after a decision to decommission it, but its capability for timing remains (with considerable advocacy to expand and use it). The rest of the discussion to follow will emphasize backup for navigation.

Usage of radar and Very High Frequency Omni Range (VOR) for commercial plus GA routing and approaches won't end any time soon, but more traffic will drive the need for improvement. Rather than better radars and VORs, an alternative or supplement - integration - has been insufficiently employed for decades. Again, once the industry stops insisting on working with position fixes, integration methods offer far superior performance. In addition to inertial integration, that holds true for measurements from GPS, radar, VOR, distance measuring equipment (DME), or any other source. Huge benefits await.

In post-NextGen, unavailability of satellite navigation again necessitates acceptance of reduced performance from alternate information sources. TCAS, for example, would be a logical backup for the improved CA described earlier in this report. Additionally, visual sources (cameras, Lidar) have produced impressive results [57] under restrictive conditions (short-range, limited atmospheric obstruction), but their role in safety-of-life operation is not yet clear (bugs can smear a sensor, partially or temporarily blinding it).

Appendix 5: Integrity Test ("Spiders in the Woodpile") [82]

RTCA Special Committee SC-159 included a working group for integrity. Much was accomplished [83] but a number of unresolved issues left both co-chairmen dissatisfied - to the extent of declining the offer to be co-authors of [83] and following it with a published comment. [84, 85] Space limitations allow only a brief summary here; among the issues causing discontent by the co-chairmen were

- Simulations with pseudocode instead of end-to-end test requirements
- Absence of demand to check for failures that were known to occur previously
- Reliance on suppliers' results instead of a standard algorithm and test
- No blind testing in mixed-trial sequences with correct outcomes unknown to the tester
- Coordinate parameters known to be integer valued used in test (Why give that hint?)
- Acceptance of statistical confidence as low as 50 percent
- No rejection, nor even retest, of receivers with catastrophic errors
- Insufficient importance attached to certification improperly bestowed

The last item, applicable at the time to the first certified GPS receiver (page 5 of [86]), was followed by spectacular discrepancies in subsequent tests performed on multiple certified GPS receivers. [87] Another flaw arises from a fundamental difference. In flight, ground truth is inaccessible; yes-or-no (GO / NO GO) logic governs (e.g., execute approach or missed approach). A receiver being tested, however, processes measurements made from known conditions. Since the amount of error is known, then GO / NO GO testing squanders effectiveness. Consider this basic limitation with a maximum number N of missed detections allowed - irrespective of whether the discrepancies are trivial or huge amounts - in the following hypothetical outcome from a large number of trial runs for two receivers:

#1 produces N missed detections, each with errors vastly beyond allowable levels.

Accept

#2 produces N + 1 missed detections, each with errors slightly above allowable levels.

Reject

It is essential for post-NextGen to avoid flawed decision-making. [86]

Appendix 6: Modern Estimation Methods Are Covered

The tonnage of publications on optimal recursive (Kalman) estimation (and its counterpart, weighted least squares via block processing, plus various extensions) is "enough to sink a battleship." Among them can be found tracts that are too pessimistic (belaboring possibilities of divergence) and many others too glib (e.g., presenting simulation results that make no allowance for imperfect modeling). Consequently, it is prudent to reassure that hard realities have been addressed, thoroughly analyzed, documented with no proprietary strings, used in designs, and verified with in-flight data [46, 47, 88].

Dates of pertinent references range all the way from the early 1960s [89] to the new satnav handbook edition [90] which contains a section showing the methods and results for precise velocity discussed in Appendix 10, along with a program for setting process noise spectral density levels discussed next.

Over a variety of diverse applications (satellite attitude determination, orbit determination, precise pointing, bit synchronization, tightly coupled GPS/inertial integration, shape states for imaging, flexural deformations of a nonrigid satellite, tracking via radar or optical sensors, etc.) [88], matrix math has been the easy part. Each operation has its own individual departures from the others. That's been invariably true even within subsets of the items just listed. For example, tracking subdivides into different modes - surface-to-air, air-to-air, air-to-surface (the latter further divisible for ships versus land vehicles not restricted to sea level) - and into several application dependent categories including short-range projectiles, high-performance fighters, passenger aircraft, reentry vehicles, satellites, missiles, land vehicles constrained to paved surfaces, etc.

With matrix math being the easy part, what's the hardest? Quite often it's the process noise. Spectral densities are difficult to harmonize with intuition. How many knots squared per Hz, propagated into subsequent position error, will produce an intended response? How many g's squared per Hz are needed to drive the velocity variance? In addition to design struggles, their covariance propagation also dominates the computation load of many Kalman filter algorithms.

This solution has worked in every application where it's been tried. Recognize that, with inevitable model imperfections, measurement data should influence estimates for only a limited duration. Rather than choosing process noise levels, set a nominal time T for that time period. Spectral density values can be quantified based on that setting. Current estimates will then be based effectively on influence of data from present time t back to time (t-T); verification and testing for different values of T are shown in [90, 91].

Remaining appendices address integration issues not familiar to all.

Appendix 7: Navigation and Tracking Similarities and Differences

Years of experience have shown, not surprisingly, appreciable overlap between navigation and tracking. Many of the same functions are performed for each operation, but there are differences. The goal of navigation in this context is to determine the state (e.g., position, velocity, etc.), often with an Earth-based origin. In air-to-air tracking, "ownship" is the customary origin, while position and velocity are relative. For multitarget tracking in crowded airspace, each aircraft needs to know every other tracked object's position and velocity relative to ownship. For that purpose, it is helpful to envision a relnav grid, wherein "absolute" (here, latitude and longitude) location is of secondary importance for making guidance decisions in heavy traffic.

A few additional clarifications are covered only briefly here with reliance on references (e.g., [47]) for elaboration. Terminology notwithstanding, nothing of interest in this report is a "target" in a military sense - though a rogue UAS could arouse some similar considerations. There is wide algorithmic variation for types of objects being tracked. For the types within scope here, differences are likely to arise from maneuverability. In those cases, states will also include tracked objects' acceleration (total, not relative since ownship maneuver modeling is adequately known). Models for target acceleration may range from fairly accurate (communicated intent) to very loose (random with band limiting, valid for short intervals only). Algorithms for all cases are known to within adjustments in logic and parameter values. [59, 92]

Under constant course conditions the tracker's knowledge of current velocity for an intruder (another aircraft), relative to ownship, enables determination of both time and separation distance at closest approach. Figure 5 plots, up to closest approach, two flight paths with collision averted by a 39-knot speed adjustment two minutes ahead of time. [54] Speed change keeps their minimum separation (logarithmically scaled in Figure 6) at one kilometer, after which separation abruptly begins to increase. In operation of course

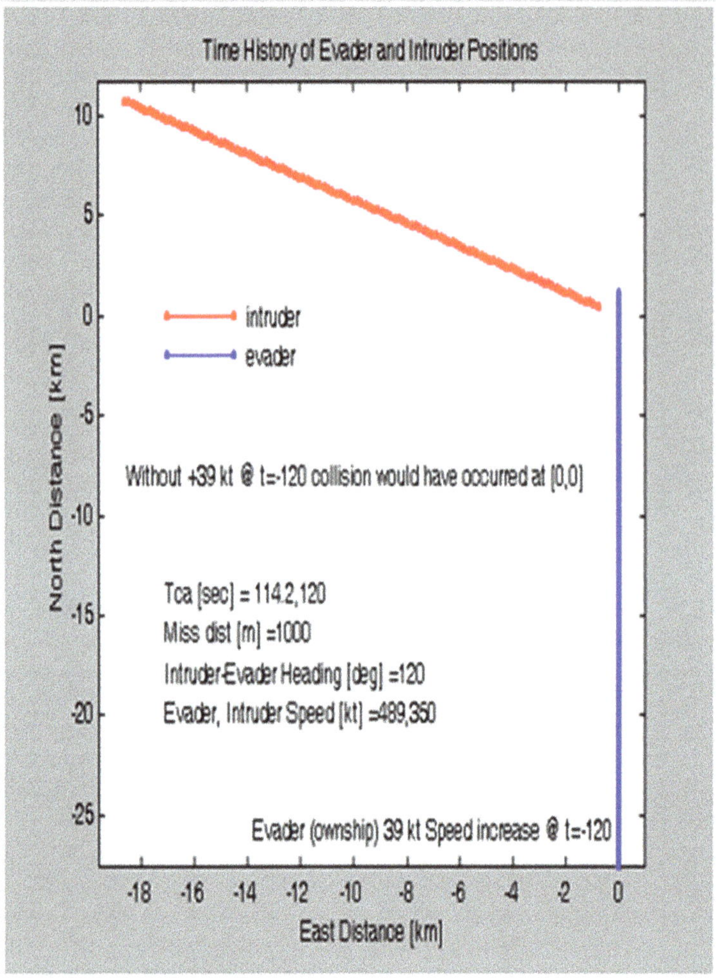

FIGURE 5. This plots, up to closest approach, two flight paths with collision averted by a 39-knot speed adjustment two minutes ahead of time.

the speed increase could not be sudden but would be spread over time (e.g., less than 0.1 g for a half minute), followed by repetitive low-level trimming to absorb updated information. Also, when both participants are aware, adjustments can be shared (one speeds up as the other slows down). More complex scenarios are discussed in J. Tang's *Conflict Detection and Resolution for Civil Aviation: A Literature Survey* [63].

Appendix 8: How Much Modeling Error Is Excessive?

Literature can be found severely critical of linearization, even as applied to the pseudorange equation. That concern is easily allayed. With an Earth-centered, Earth-fixed (ECEF) reference used, initial position can be placed at the geocenter (or even at the opposite side of the Earth from true location) and convergence is reached after three weighted least squares iterations. Processing can continue by recursion thereafter, with emphasis given to the most recent observations as discussed at the end of Appendix 6. The practice is fitting data to a model, which - for multiple reasons (e.g., nonlinearities, inexactly known parameters) - is imperfect. Success is achieved because perfect models are not required.

Still, the theory is based on idealized conditions. Various practical ways have evolved to cope with departures from idealization. Acceptance criteria for deviations can be based on a simple question of whether the effect is smaller than the impact of random or other uncorrectable errors present. *GNSS Aided Navigation & Tracking: Inertially Augmented or Autonomous* [47, section 2.9] offers details for those wishing to pursue this further.

Appendix 9: Transmitted Measurements with Respect to Center of Gravity

A high-precision requirement raises the topic of a structure's specific sites: it is pointless to demand centimeter position

FIGURE 6. Speed change keeps their minimum separation (logarithmically scaled) at one kilometer, after which separation abruptly begins to increase.

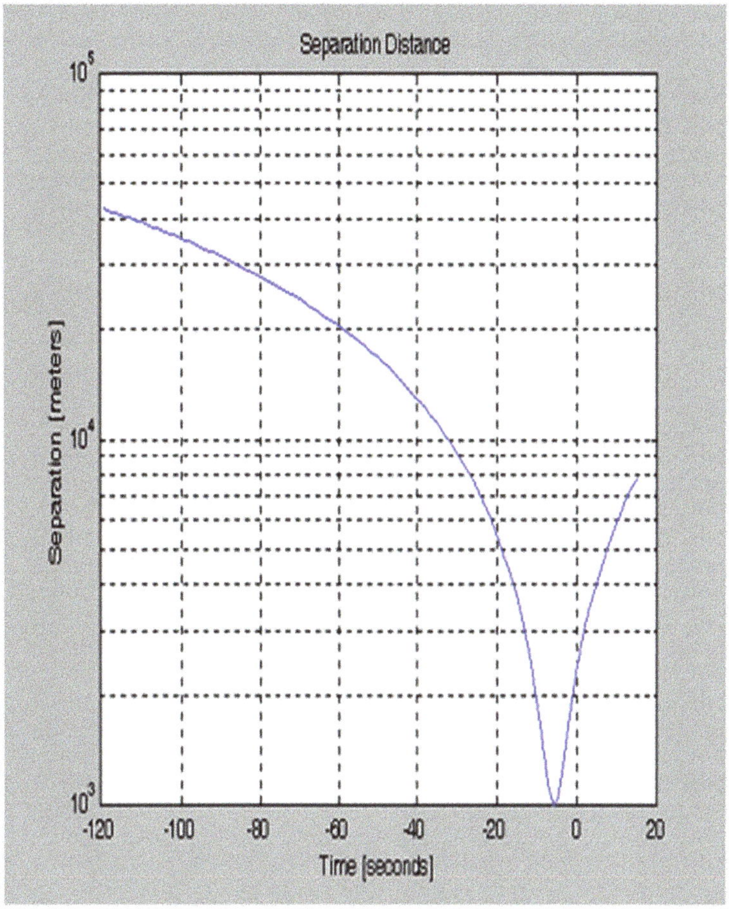

accuracy for aircraft with 20-meter wingspan moving at 400 knots. For velocity, though, that subject advances another issue more subtle. Cockpit experience will not match velocity history of the nose or tail which undulate in opposite phase with fluctuating rotations. With the center of gravity (c-g) moving in a smooth arc (Figure 7a), other sites will then exhibit a wavy path (Figure 7b). Samples from a time trace of velocity experienced by a sensor off c-g will exhibit unwanted effects. Those distractions hamper efforts to fit an arc through the sample points, degrading accuracy that is meant to be precise. Transmitted sequential increments in carrier phase, then, should be adjusted to extract the lever arm effect off c-g. Likewise, values obtained from messages should be compared against increments adjusted for lever arm effect at the received end.

Appendix 10: High Accuracy in Velocity without High Accuracy in Position

With nominal 20-centimeter L-band wavelength, an 18-degree phase detector error yields just one centimeter position error. Although many impressive successes have been achieved, risk of an occasional undetected cycle slip produces a well-known catastrophic result. The huge (satellite-to-receiver distance/wavelength) multiple must consistently have accuracy better than one part in a hundred million to avoid incorrect ambiguity resolution. Subtracting two ambiguous phases one second apart reduces the multiple to manageable values while sacrificing the position determination capability. Instead, differencing produces a velocity component having that centimeter/second accuracy amplified by factors of 1.414 - with no catastrophic risk and no need to resolve cycle ambiguity - ever. Additionally, it brings the following benefits:

- Incremental cycle count error would be glaring, enabling prompt rejection
- Uncertain cycle count could be used with variance set to exceed (wavelength^2)
- Measurement acceptability is easily based on rigorous integrity methodology
- SV data can be discontinuous; usage resumes as integrity test is satisfied
- In the limit, the preceding trait even allows usage of fragmented data

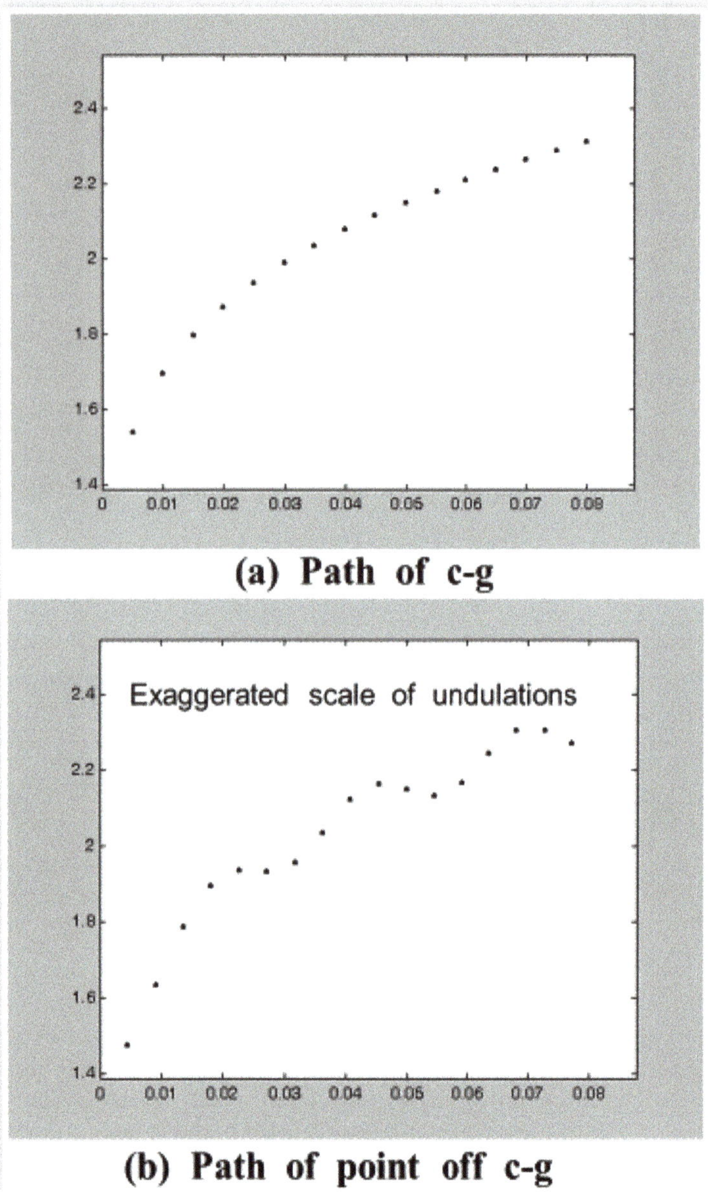

FIGURE 7. Cockpit experience will not match velocity history of the nose or tail which undulate in opposite phase with fluctuating rotations. With the center of gravity (c-g) moving in a smooth arc, other sites will then exhibit a wavy path.

- No mask is needed; small effects of iono and tropo changes are largely known
- The preceding item enables using observations all the way down to horizon
- Low elevation SV usage (newly visible or sinking) enhances geometric spread
- Ephemeris error effects on the dynamics segment are negligible
- Interoperability; constellation mismatch has negligible effect on dynamics

Accounting for all effects (e.g., satellite motion, etc.) during the differencing interval is not trivial but quite manageable. Details for navigation appear in Position Navigation & Timing technologies in the 21st Century [90] and GNSS Aided Navigation & Tracking: Inertially Augmented or Autonomous [47], and details for tracking appear in Flight Test Results of a Measurement-Based ADS-B System for Separation Assurance [46].

Appendix 11: "Unlikely" Isn't a Strong Enough Condition

"One chance in a million" sounds remote but warrants reconsideration. With several thousand passenger aircraft in the sky each

FIGURE 8. Simple programs summing weighted gaussian inputs readily show how serious the effect can be: even ten-sigma events, although unusual, can't be discounted.

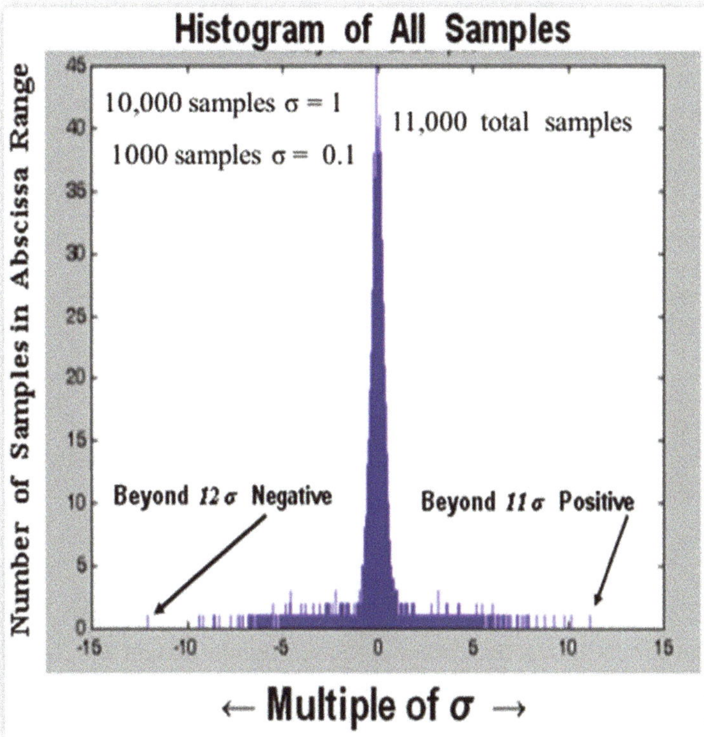

day worldwide (almost 4,000 in U.S. alone), multiplied by 365 days per year - assuming two takeoffs and landings on average for each flight - then the number of critical flight phases per year is well over six million. Then a one-in-a-million chance for a collision would imply six collisions per year. Admittedly, these figures are highly speculative, even glib, but they serve to illustrate a point: It is insufficient for a collision to be "unlikely" - the requirement to be unlikely enough has spawned much detailed risk assessment. The significance of these considerations is further amplified by another issue, addressed next.

Ramifications of Inapplicable Gaussian Models

There are multiple criteria for defining "optimum" estimates (e.g., maximum likelihood, median, minimum variance). In many cases they produce different answers. Nevertheless, a Kalman filter provides minimum variance estimates in a linear system (and near minimum variance in a properly designed linearized one), regardless of (often unknown) random inputs' probability distributions. Recognition of minimum variance as a valid goal enables versatility of design methods without restriction to gaussian inputs, as long as it is realized that distribution tails are not tight; an explanation follows.

To many minds, it is second nature to translate mentally from 2σ or 3σ to probability .95 or .997, respectively. Without knowing actual distributions, we may rationalize ("anyway the central limit theorem tends toward gaussian..."). There is wide accession - but insufficient adherence in designs - to the danger of assuming very low probabilities for places out on the tails of a distribution. Reality is often characterized by "fat tails," even for much-higher-than-usual multiples of σ.

One reason for missing that point is a common oversight. Except for only the most elementary situations, "gaussian in, gaussian out" does not apply, even in perfectly linear systems where all random inputs are gaussian. Those outputs are mixed gaussian. Simple programs summing weighted gaussian inputs readily show how serious the effect can be: even ten-sigma events, although unusual, can't be discounted (Figure 8). Some recent investigations applied Extreme Value Theory to the 2007 financial crisis with the value at risk expressed in dollars. For greater relevance to our field, *Containment Limits for Free-Inertial Coast* [93] defined the value at risk as navigation error accumulated through error propagation.

Additional Ramifications from Another Direction

It is widely recognized that receiver software problems are far more prevalent than signal-in-space failures. Conditions described in preceding material prompted a voicing of this question in a 2000 Legal Issues Panel: [94]

> *"Given the awareness of this situation as well as the existence of documentation providing an example of misinterpreted certification test procedures, what are the liability implications for FAA, for the airlines, for the airframe manufacturers, and for the equipment suppliers in the event of an accident?"*

The reference cited also documents the absence of any recorded answer. Only a verbal comment was offered - "That's not a new problem." - prompting an obvious realization: "Not new" is all the more reason why reaction should have been planned. Complacency can be fatal, especially now with airspace shared by both manned and unmanned aircraft.

While legal issues addressed here are necessarily limited, one additional item deserves stress. UAS operation can either provide vital capabilities (e.g., search and rescue) or be eroded by leniency toward abusers. Those alternatives are mutually exclusive; sanctions need to be swift and severe.

SAE EDGE™ Research Reports

SAE EDGE™ Research Reports, like the present report on "Unsettled Topics in the Application of Satellite Navigation to Air Traffic Management," are intended to push further out into still unsettled areas of technology of interest to the mobility industry. SAE launches these reports before attempting to form a joint working group, let alone a cooperative research program or a standards committee.

SAE EDGE™ reports are intended to be quick, concise overviews of major unsettled areas where vital new technologies are emerging. An unsettled area is characterized more by confusion and controversy than established order. Early practitioners must confront an absence of agreement. Their challenge is often not to seize the high ground but to find common ground. These scouting reports from the frontiers of investigation are intended merely to begin the process of sorting through critical issues, contributing to a better understanding of key problems, and providing helpful suggestions about possible next steps and avenues of investigation.

SAE EDGE™ Research Reports, therefore, are fundamentally distinct from the more formal working groups approach and far removed from the more mature research program and standard's development process.

Next Steps for the Application of Satellite Navigation to Air Traffic Management

This publication is a first step toward clarifying the issues around ATM. The intention behind this and other SAE EDGE™ Research Reports is to start a dialogue among interested parties on important industry-wide topics that require further attention. The expectation is that these explorations of unsettled areas of technology will lead to the formation of working groups and, ultimately, committees that can address and resolve the issues they raise, producing a framework for developing a common vocabulary of definitions, best practices, protocols, and standards needed to support continued progress toward safer and more innovative products.

SAE International has demonstrated its lead in this and closely related areas by the advocacy presented before the National PNT Advisory Board [51, 53] plus standards committees led by William Woodward, Chairman, SAE International Aerospace Avionics Systems Division.

This SAE EDGE™ Research Report on "Unsettled Topics in the Application of Satellite Navigation to Air Traffic Management" identifies the following key topics for further pursuit, both through continued informal discussions among industry practitioners and through more formal working groups:

- Review flight operations in light of known NextGen problems, increased traffic density, and UAS proliferation.
- Heed the urgent demands for vigilance in the presence of increasingly severe interference.
- Realize that operational systems currently lack vital authentication and adequate integrity verification and take corrective steps.
- Face the reality that dense traffic will make position fixes increasingly impotent for providing safe separation and cease dependence on full-fix position pseudomeasurements.
- Recognize the paramount importance of accurate dynamics over instantaneous location and express requirements accordingly.
- Multiple complications impose requirements for innovations. Higher traffic density and presence of UASs call for development of guidance strategies not requiring abrupt climb/dive for CA. Worsening interference necessitates continued APNT development for reduced operation using backup information in the absence of satnav data.
- Recognize both (1) the wisdom gained from automatic pilot override already achieved and (2) how Air Force tradition differs from passenger airline experience. Account for that in planned developments.
- Reasons for inaction or delay (e.g., from administrative inertia, old habits, outdated procedures, turf battles, divergent opinions, unawareness of applicable principles, misdirected goals, business models for maximizing profits) must cease to govern.

Recommendations

The overall recommendations of this SAE EDGE™ Research Report can be summarized as follows:

1. Correct the known NextGen problems already identified and expand to include further discrepancies.

2. Make vigilance the rule rather than the exception. Follow through with actions being undertaken to address the long-standing need for backup in GNSS-denied environments.
3. Adopt measures already devised and under further test for authentication. Correct known flaws in verification of integrity.
4. Make availability of raw measurements mandatory for data sharing via communications.
5. Capitalize on all the well-known (for decades) performance enhancements unchained by the availability of raw measurement data.
6. Exploit the dramatic improvements just noted in devising guidance strategies to cope with higher traffic. Always include preparation for transition into reduced operation with relaxed requirements prescribed for backup provisions used in the absence of satnav data.
7. Upcoming developments in automation, though unforeseeable, may be envisioned with a measured phased-in approach.
8. Establish a management group of limited size having responsibility to define plans plus authority to implement all requisite steps. Since urgency is a major factor, there is a need to expedite in ways unprecedented for civil aviation. Cooperation will be needed across the board, with awareness by relevant institutions within government, industry, academia, and professional organizations.

Definitions

3D - Three Dimensions/Three-Dimensional
AACAS - Automatic Air Collision Avoidance System
ACAS - Airborne Collision Avoidance System
ADS-B - Automatic Dependent Surveillance - Broadcast
AGCAS - Automatic Ground Collision Avoidance System
AI - Artificial Intelligence
APNT - Alternative Positioning, Navigation, and Timing
ATM - Air Traffic Management
BVLOS - Beyond Visual Line Of Sight
c-g - Center of Gravity
CA - Collision Avoidance
CFR - Code of Federal Regulations
DGPS - Differential Global Positioning System
EKF - Extended Kalman Filter
ES - Extended Squitter
EU - European Union
FAA - Federal Aviation Administration
FAR - Federal Acquisition Regulation
FCC - Federal Communications Commission
FIS-B - Flight Information Services - Broadcast
FRP - Federal Radionavigation Plan
FSS - Flight Service Station
GA - General Aviation
GNSS - Global Navigation Satellite System
GPS - Global Positioning System
ICAO - International Civil Aviation Organization
IEEE - Institute of Electrical and Electronics Engineers
ION - Institute of Navigation
ISO - International Organization for Standardization
LEO - Low Earth Orbiter
LTE - Long-Term Evolution
NAS - National Airspace System
PNT - Positioning, Navigation, and Timing
PPP - Precise Point Positioning
RA - Resolution Advisories
RAIM - Receiver Autonomous Integrity Monitoring
RNP - Required Navigation Performance
RNTF - Resilient Navigation and Timing Foundation
RTK - Real Time Kinematic
sUAS - small Unmanned Aircraft Systems
SV - Space Vehicle
TA - Traffic Alerts
TBO - Trajectory Based Operations
TCA - Time of Closest Approach
TCAS - Traffic Collision Avoidance System
TIS-B - Traffic Information Services - Broadcast
UAS - Unmanned Aircraft Systems
UASSC - Unmanned Aircraft Systems Standardization Collaborative
UAT - Universal Access Transceiver
UTM - UAS Traffic Management
VFR - Visual Flight Rule
VOR - Very High Frequency Omni Range

Acknowledgements

Recognition should go first to all the participants, many of who also provided feedback on the draft version of this publication. Without their input and initiative, this SAE EDGE™ Research Report would not have been possible.

Dana A. Goward, Resilient Navigation and Timing Foundation and Maritime Governance, LLC
Dorota Grejner-Brzezinska, Ph.D., Ohio State University College of Engineering
Tim Murphy, Boeing
Maj. Ron Ogan, Civil Air Patrol
Logan Scott, Logan Scott Consulting
Doug Taggart, Overlook Systems Technologies, Inc.
Erik Theunissen, Ph.D., Netherlands Defence Academy
Maarten Uijt de Haag, Ph.D., Technische Universität Berlin
William Woodward, SAE International Aerospace Avionics Systems Division

Additional thanks go to the following individuals who also had the opportunity to provide feedback on the draft version of this publication. Their contributions helped shape this publication.

Dr. Joseph Lyons
Air Force Research Laboratory

Robert W. Lilley, Ph.D.
Aviation Management Associates, Inc.

The authors of this document together with the SAE Team responsible for its creation join in expressing our deepest appreciation to all the individuals mentioned above.

References

1. Blanch, J., Walter, T., and Enge, P., "Satellite Navigation for Aviation in 2025," *Proceedings of the IEEE* 100(Special Centennial Issue):1821-1830, 2012. https://doi.org/10.1109/jproc.2012.2190154.
2. Class, K.A., Hartman, R.G., and Helgeson, B.J., "Differential GPS Landing Assistance System," Google Patents US5361212A, Google, https://patents.google.com/patent/US5361212A/en, accessed January 17, 2020.
3. Parkinson, B., Doherty, J., Darrah, J., Donahue, A., Hirsch, L., Jewell, D., Klepczynski, W. et al., "Independent Assessment Team (IAT) Summary of Initial Findings on ELoran," Institute for Defense Analyses, Alexandria, VA, 2009, https://rosap.ntl.bts.gov/view/dot/16939, accessed April 7, 2020.
4. Federal Aviation Administration, "Loran's Capability to Mitigate the Impact of a GPS Outage on GPS Position, Navigation, and Time Applications Prepared for the Federal Aviation Administration," Vice President for Technical Operations Navigation Services Directorate, Washington, D.C., 2004, https://rntfnd.org/wp-content/uploads/FAA-Report-2004-Lorans-Capability-to-Mitigate-the-Impact-of-a-GPS-Outage-on-GPS-PNT-Applications.pdf, accessed April 7, 2020.
5. Office of the Secretary (OST), U.S. Department of Transportation (DOT), "Positioning, Navigation, and Timing (PNT) Service for National Critical Infrastructure Resiliency [DOT-OST-2016-0227]," Federal Register 81, no. 230, November 30, 2016, 86378-80. https://www.federalregister.gov/documents/2016/11/30/2016-28805/positioning-navigation-and-timing-pnt-service-for-national-critical-infrastructure-resiliency, accessed April 7, 2020.
6. Volpe, J.A. and Center, N.T.S., *Vulnerability Assessment of the Transportation Infrastructure Relying on the Global Positioning System* (Cambridge, MA: Department of Transportation, 2001). https://www.hsdl.org/?abstract&did=1815, accessed April 7, 2020.
7. Kovach, K. and Conley, R., "SATZAP: A Novel Approach to GPS Integrity*," *Navigation* 38(2):163-190, 1991. https://doi.org/10.1002/j.2161-4296.1991.tb01722.x.
8. YouTube, "Navy Strike Rescue," https://youtu.be/1ORCAY-B9mk, accessed January 15, 2020.
9. SEBoK, "Federal Aviation Administration (FAA) Next Generation Air Transportation System: Semantic Scholar," Federal Aviation Administration (FAA) Next Generation Air Transportation System, Semantic Scholar, June 2, 2019, https://www.semanticscholar.org/paper/Federal-Aviation-Administration-(-FAA-)-Next-Air-SEBoK/cbe33db94f83a489acff93e12adcfbcfd6976669, accessed April 7, 2020.
10. Halsey, A. III, "FAA Bungles $36 Billion NextGen Aviation Project, Federal Report Says," *The Seattle Times*, The Seattle Times Company, March 9, 2018, https://www.seattletimes.com/nation-world/inspector-generals-report-says-the-faa-has-bungled-a-36-billion-project/, accessed April 7, 2020.
11. Aviation Week Network, "NextGen Reality Check: Problems Persist as FAA Installs Framework: Aviation Week Network," May 24, 2018, https://aviationweek.com/commercial-aviation/nextgen-reality-check-problems-persist-faa-installs-framework, accessed April 7, 2020.
12. Beukers, J., "Status of Worldwide Radionavigation," in *Proceedings of the 2001 National Technical Meeting of The Institute of Navigation*, Long Beach, CA, January 2001, 1-24.
13. Costin, A. and Francillon, A., "Ghost Is in the Air (Traffic)," Presentation at the *USA Blackhat Conference*, Las Vegas, NV, 2012.
14. Narins, M.J., Eldredge, L.V., Enge, P., Lo, S.C. et al., "Alternative Position, Navigation, and Timing: The Need for Robust Radionavigation," in *Global Navigation Satellite Systems, Report of a Joint Workshop of the National Academy of Engineering and the Chinese Academy of Engineering* (Washington, D.C.: The National Academics Press, 2012), 119-136.
15. Hauschild, A., Tegedor, J., Montenbruck, O., Visser, H., and Markgraf, M., "Orbit Determination of LEO Satellites with Real-Time Corrections," GPS World, April 24, 2017, https://www.gpsworld.com/innovation-orbit-determination-of-leo-satellites-with-real-time-corrections/, accessed April 7, 2020.
16. Farrell, J.L., "Loose Coupling - And What's Wrong With It," GPS World, January 2, 2015, https://www.gpsworld.com/expert-advice-loose-coupling-and-whats-wrong-with-it/, accessed April 7, 2020.
17. "Automatic Dependent Surveillance-Broadcast (ADS-B) Out Equipment and Use," Doc. No. FAA-2007-29305, 75 FR 30193, May 28, 2010; Amdt. 91-314-A, 75 FR 37712, June 30, 2010, https://www.govinfo.gov/content/pkg/CFR-2011-title14-vol2/pdf/CFR-2011-title14-vol2-sec91-225.pdf, accessed April 7, 2020.
18. Bergqvist, P., "FAA Cracks Down on Erroneous ADS-B Codes," Flying, https://www.flyingmag.com/faa-cracks-down-on-erroneous-ads-b-codes/, accessed January 15, 2020.
19. Federal Aviation Administration, "FAA Safety Briefing," March/April 2017, https://www.faa.gov/news/safety_briefing/2017/media/MarApr2017.pdf, accessed April 7, 2020.

20. Federal Aviation Administration, "Public ADS-B Performance Report (PAPR) User's Guide," November 2019, https://adsbperformance.faa.gov/PAPRUsersGuide.pdf, accessed April 7, 2020.
21. FAA Seal, "Commercial Operations Branch," September 27, 2018, https://www.faa.gov/about/office_org/headquarters_offices/avs/offices/afx/afs/afs800/afs820/part107_oper/, accessed April 7, 2020.
22. Federal Aviation Administration, "Unmanned Aircraft Systems Safety Risk Management Policy," April 10, 2019. https://www.faa.gov/documentLibrary/media/Order/FAA_Order_8040.6.pdf, accessed April 7, 2020
23. European Union Aviation Safety Agency RMT.0230, "High-Level Regulatory Framework for the U-Space," Draft Opinion in accordance with Art. 16 (Accelerated procedure) of MB Decision No. 18-2015, 2020.
24. JARUS, "JARUS Guidelines on Specific Operations Risk Assessment (SORA)," Document JAR-DEL-WG6-D.04, Edition 1.0, June 26, 2017.
25. Feuer, W., "New Rule Would Make It Possible to Track and Identify Nearly All Drones Flying in the U.S.," CNBC, December 26, 2019, https://www.cnbc.com/2019/12/26/faa-remote-id-rule-for-drones-would-enable-tracking-identification.html, accessed April 7, 2020.
26. Federal Aviation Administration, "Remote Identification of Unmanned Aircraft Systems," December, 26, 2019, https://s3.amazonaws.com/public-inspection.federalregister.gov/2019-28100.pdf, accessed April 7, 2020.
27. Homeland Security Today, "UN Aviation Body: GPS/GNSS Disruption an Urgent Safety Priority," December 12, 2019, https://www.hstoday.us/subject-matter-areas/transportation/un-aviation-body-gps-gnss-disruption-an-urgent-safety-priority/, accessed April 7, 2020.
28. Hughes, D., "Jam Busters," ATT01SEP2019, http://journal-download.co.uk/digitalmagazines/ATT/ATT01SEP2019/page_41.html, accessed January 15, 2020.
29. Times of Israel, "Disruption of GPS Systems at Ben Gurion Airport Resolved after 2 Months," August 5, 2019, https://www.timesofisrael.com/disruption-of-gps-systems-at-ben-gurion-airport-resolved-after-2-months/, accessed April 7, 2020.
30. Niles, R.. "'GPS Signals Sometimes Jammed. Check before You Go, or Else…' - FAA," RNTF, July 16, 2019, https://rntfnd.org/2019/07/16/gps-signals-sometimes-jammed-check-before-you-go-or-else-faa/, accessed April 7, 2020.
31. Fearn, N., "Hackers Can Fake Radio Signals to Hijack Aircraft Landing Systems, Warn Researchers: Computing," May 16, 2019, https://www.computing.co.uk/ctg/news/3075890/hackers-aircraft-landing-fake-radio-signals, accessed April 7, 2020.
32. Goward, D., "NASA Report: Passenger Aircraft Nearly Crashes Due GPS Disruption - GPS World," RNTF, July 9, 2019, https://rntfnd.org/2019/07/09/nasa-report-passenger-aircraft-nearly-crashes-due-gps-disruption-gps-world/, accessed April 7, 2020.
33. Lilley, R., Church, G., and Harrison, M., "GPS Backup For Position, Navigation and Timing Transition Strategy for Navigation and Surveillance," Aviation Management Associates, Inc. White Paper for FAA, August 22, 2006.
34. SESAR, "High Performing Aviation for Europe," Web page, SESAR Joint Undertaking, 2019, https://www.sesarju.eu/, accessed April 7, 2020.
35. STRIKE3 Project, "STRIKE3 - Monitor, Detect, Characterise, Standardize, Mitigate and Protect," Web page, STRIKE3, 2019, http://www.gnss-strike3.eu/, accessed April 7, 2020.
36. STRIKE3_D42_TestStandards, "Standardization of GNSS Threat Reporting and Receiver Testing Through International Knowledge Exchange, Experimentation and Exploitation Strike3," Issue 3.0, January, 25, 2019, http://www.aic-aachen.org/strike3/downloads/STRIKE3_D4.2_Test_Standards_v3.0_public.pdf, accessed April 7, 2020.
37. Logan Scott Consulting, "CHIMERA Specification," http://www.gpsexpert.net/chimera-specification, accessed January 15, 2020.
38. Homeland Security, "Improving the Operation and Development of Global Positioning System (GPS) Equipment Used by Critical Infrastructure," https://www.us-cert.gov/sites/default/files/documents/Improving_the_Operation_and_Development_of_Global_Positioning_System_%28GPS%29_Equipment_Used_by_Critical_Infrastructure_S508C.pdf, accessed April 7, 2020.
39. McGraw, G.A., "Toughening GPS Receivers Against Interference: Ensuring Signal Reception in Spectrally Busy Environments," in *National Space-Based Positioning, Navigation, and Timing Advisory Board, 14th Meeting*, Washington, DC, December 10, 2014, https://www.gps.gov/governance/advisory/meetings/2014-12/mcgraw.pdf, accessed April 7, 2020.
40. Stratton, A. and Weger, J., "Anti-Jamming for Airborne Platforms," in *National Space-Based Positioning, Navigation, and Timing Advisory Board, 21st Meeting*, Baltimore, MD, May, 2018, https://www.gps.gov/governance/advisory/meetings/2018-05/stratton.pdf, accessed April 7, 2020.
41. Scott, L., "An Observation On Using Foreign GNSS in Critical Applications," LinkedIn, https://www.linkedin.com/pulse/observation-using-foreign-gnss-critical-applications-logan-scott/, accessed January 15, 2020.
42. von Sickle, G.A., "GPS for Military Surveillance," GPS World, November 1996.

43. Farrell, J.L., Mcconkey, E.D., and Gary Stephens, C., "Send Measurements, Not Coordinates," *Navigation* 46(3):203-215, 1999. https://doi.org/10.1002/j.2161-4296.1999.tb02407.x.

44. Farrell, J.L., "Send Measurements, Not Coordinates," *Institute of Navigation Newsletter* 26(3):14-15, Summer 2016. https://www.ion.org/publications/upload/v26n3.pdf, accessed April 7, 2020.

45. Farrell, J.L. "Enabling Collision Avoidance with Raw Measurements and Updated ADS-B Software," Inside GNSS, November 20, 2019, https://insidegnss.com/enabling-collision-avoidance-with-raw-measurements-and-updated-ads-b-software/. https://insidegnss.com/wp-content/uploads/2018/01/julyaug17-FARRELL.pdf, accessed April 7, 2020.

46. Duan, P., Ujit de Haag, M., and Farrell, J.L., "Flight Test Results of a Measurement-Based ADS-B System for Separation Assurance," *Navigation, Journal of the Institute of Navigation* 60(3):221-234, 2013. https://doi.org/10.1002/navi.41.

47. Farrell, J.L., *GNSS Aided Navigation and Tracking -- Inertially Augmented or Autonomous* (Baltimore, MD: American Literary Press, 2007).

48. Barhydt, R., Eischeid, T.M., Palmer, M.T., and Wing, D.J., "Use Of A Prototype Airborne Separation Assurance System for Resolving Near-Term Conflicts during Autonomous Aircraft Operations," 2003, AIAA 2003-5401.

49. Farrell, J.L., "Keeping Pace with Avionics Innovations," in *Proceedings of the IEEE 1977 National Aerospace and Electronics Conference, NAECON77*, 1282-1289, IEEE - Institute of Electrical and Electronics Engineers, Dayton OH, May 17-19, 1977.

50. Gopalapillai, G.S., Ruck, G.T., and Mourad, A.G., "Satellite Interferometer as an Advanced Navigation/Communication System," *Navigation, Journal of the Institute of Navigation* 25(4):405-418, 1978.

51. Farrell, J.L., "Interface Requirements for SAE-Compliant GPS Receivers," in *National Space-Based Positioning, Navigation, and Timing Advisory Board, 21st Meeting*, Baltimore, MD, May 17, 2018. https://www.gps.gov/governance/advisory/meetings/2018-05/farrell.pdf, accessed April 7, 2020.

52. Farrell, J.L., "Raw Data to Improve Accuracy, Integrity, & Availability of SatNav," in *National Space-Based Positioning, Navigation, and Timing Advisory Board, 15th Meeting*, Annapolis, MD, June 11, 2015, https://www.gps.gov/governance/advisory/meetings/2015-06/farrell.pdf, accessed April 7, 2020.

53. Woodward, B., "Proposed Guidelines For Resilient Pnt Receivers," in *National Space-Based Positioning, Navigation, And Timing Advisory Board, 23rd Meeting*, Alexandria, VA, June 6, 2019, https://www.gps.gov/governance/advisory/meetings/2019-06/woodward.pdf. https://insidegnss.com/wp-content/uploads/2018/01/julyaug17-FARRELL.pdf, accessed April 7, 2020.

54. Farrell, J.L., "Collision Avoidance by Speed Change," *Coordinates* VIII(9):8-12, September 2012. https://mycoordinates.org/collision-avoidance-by-speed-change/, accessed April 7, 2020.

55. ANSI, "Unmanned Aircraft Systems Standardization Collaborative (UASSC)," https://share.ansi.org/Shared%20Documents/Standards%20Activities/UASSC/UASSC_Participating_Organizations.pdf, accessed April 7, 2020.

56. ISO, "ISO/TC 20/SC 16 - Unmanned Aircraft Systems," March 8, 2017, https://www.iso.org/committee/5336224.html, accessed April 7, 2020.

57. Dill, E.T. and Ujit de Haag, M., "3D Multi-Copter Navigation and Mapping Using GPS, Inertial, and LiDAR," *Navigation: Journal of the Institute of Navigation* 63(2):205-220, Summer 2016.

58. Sabatini, R., Gardi, A., Ramasamy, S., Kistan, T., and Marino, M., *Novel ATM and Avionic Systems for Environmentally Sustainable Aviation* (2014), https://doi.org/10.13140/2.1.1938.0808.

59. Farrell, J.L., "Tracking: Cartesian vs Spherical Coordinates," James L Farrell, June 12, 2010. https://jameslfarrell.com/cartesianvsspherical/, accessed April 7, 2020.

60. Farrell, J.L., "Kalman Filter or Suboptimal - Does It Matter?," James L Farrell, June 29, 2010, https://jameslfarrell.com/kalman-filter-or-suboptimal-does-it-matter/, accessed April 7, 2020.

61. Haessig, D.A., Ogan, R.T., and Olive, M., "'Sense and Avoid' - What's required for aircraft safety?," *Proceedings of IEEE SEcon*, 2016, http://ieee-aess.org/sites/ieee-aess.org/files/documents/ID26-Sense-and-avoid-SEcon2016final4Mar2016PID4125261.pdf, accessed April 7, 2020.

62. Swierstra, S., "Lessons Learned: The Rise and Fall of the SESAR ATM Improvement Program," 2018, https://www.academia.edu/36511404/Lessons_Learned_The_Rise_and_Fall_of_the_SESAR_ATM_improvement_program, accessed April 7, 2020.

63. Tang, J., "Conflict Detection and Resolution for Civil Aviation: A Literature Survey," *IEEE Aerospace and Electronic Systems Magazine* 34(10):20-35, October 2019. https://doi.org/10.1109/MAES.2019.2914986.

64. Tadema, J., Theunissen, E., Rademaker, R.M., and Uijt de Haag, M., "Evaluating the Impact of Sensor Data Uncertainty and Maneuver Uncertainty in a Conflict Probe," in *Proceedings of the Digital Avionics Systems Conference*, Salt Lake City, UT, 2010.

65. RTCA, Inc., "Minimum Operational Performance Standards (MOPS) for Unmanned Aircraft Systems (UAS) Detect and Avoid (DAA) Systems," RTCA

Paper No. 197-15/SC228-027, Washington, D.C., July 2015.

66. General Atomics Aeronautical Systems Inc., "GA-ASI DAA System Aids FAA-Approved Flight of NASA Unmanned Aircraft," http://www.ga-asi.com/ga-asi-daa-system-aids-faa-approved-flight-of-nasa-unmanned-aircraft, accessed January 15, 2020.
67. YouTube, "The Automatic Ground Collision Avoidance System (Auto GCAS)," https://www.youtube.com/watch?v=Wf27X73jxlE, accessed January 16, 2020.
68. YouTube, "Automatic Air Collision Avoidance System (ACAS)," https://www.youtube.com/watch?v=O8AKDe1XBT0, accessed January 16, 2020.
69. SKYbrary Wiki, "Airborne Collision Avoidance System (ACAS) - SKYbrary Aviation Safety," https://www.skybrary.aero/index.php/Airborne_Collision_Avoidance_System_(ACAS), accessed January 15, 2020.
70. Hansman, J., "2019 PNT Symposium," October 30, 2019, http://web.stanford.edu/group/scpnt/pnt/PNT19/presentation_files/I04-Hansman-PNT-Civil_Aviation.pdf, accessed April 7, 2020.
71. USAF Maj. Donald L. McCallie, "Exploring Potential ADS-B Vulnerabilites in the FAA'S NextGen Air Transportation System," Dept. of Air Force Air University Graduate Research Project AFIT/ICW/ENG/11-09, Air Force Institute of Technology, Wright-Patterson Air Force Base, OH, June 2011.
72. "Urgent Need for DOD and FAA to Address Risks and Improve Planning for Technology That Tracks Military Aircraft," HOMELAND DEFENSE Report to Congressional Committees, January 2018. https://www.gao.gov/assets/690/689478.pdf, accessed April 7, 2020.
73. Sabatini, R., "Next-Generation ATM Systems: Increasing Safety, Efficiency and Sustainability of the Aviation Sector," in *Second International Conference on Sustainable Aviation (ISSA 2016)*, Istanbul, Turkey, https://www.academia.edu/26485894/Next-Generation_ATM_Systems_Increasing_Safety_Efficiency_and_Sustainability_of_the_Aviation_Sector, accessed January 16, 2020.
74. Wielgosz, P., Grejner-Brzezinska, D.A., and Kashani, I., "High-Accuracy DGPS and Precise Point Positioning Based on Ohio CORS Network," *Navigation* 52(1):23-28, 2005.
75. Wubbena, G., Schmitz M., and Bagge, A., "PPP-RTK: Precise Point Positioning Using State-Space Representation in RTK Networks," in *Proc. ION GNSS*, Long Beach, CA, September 13-16, 2005, 2584-2594.
76. Teunissen, P.J.G. and Khodabandeh, A., "Review and Principles of PPP-RTK Methods," *Journal of Geodesy* 89(3):217-240, 2014. https://doi.org/10.1007/s00190-014-0771-3.
77. Choy, S., Bisnath, S., and Rizos, C., "Uncovering Common Misconceptions in GNSS Precise Point Positioning and Its Future Prospect," *GPS Solutions* 21(1):13-22, January 2017. https://doi.org/10.1007/s10291-016-0545-x.
78. Laurichesse, D. and Banville, S., "Instantaneous Centimeter-Level Multi-Frequency Precise Point Positioning," GPS World July 4, 2018.
79. Farrell, J.L., "Robust Design for GNSS Integration," Presented at Institute of Navigation GNSS, 2008, James L Farrell, http://jameslfarrell.com/wp-content/uploads/2010/05/robust.pdf, accessed April 7, 2020.
80. Young, R.S.Y. and McGraw, G.A., "Fault Detection and Exclusion Using Normalized Solution Separation and Residual Monitoring Methods," *Navigation, Journal of the Institute of Navigation* 50(3):151-169, 2003. https://doi.org/10.1002/j.2161-4296.2003.tb00326.x.
81. Farrell, J.L., "Single-Measurement RAIM," James L Farrell, October 2, 2010, https://jameslfarrell.com/single-measurement-raim/, accessed April 7, 2020.
82. Farrell, J.L. and van Graas, F., "Statistical Validation for GPS Integrity Test," in *ION Redbook V.* (1998), 89-100.
83. Lee, Y., Van Dyke, K., DeCleene, B., Studenny, J., and Beckmann, M., "Summary of RTCA SC-159 GPS Integrity Working Group Activities," *Navigation, Journal of the Institute of Navigation* 43(3):307-338, September 1, 1996. https://www.ion.org/publications/abstract.cfm?articleID=100064.
84. Farrell, J.L. and van Graas, F., "Comments on "Summary of RTCA SC-159 GPS Integrity Working Group Activities,"," *Navigation, Journal of the Institute of Navigation* 44(4):497-498, Winter 1997-1998.
85. Lee, Y., van Dyke, K., DeCleene, B., Studenny, J., and Beckmann, M., "Authors' Reply to Comments on "Summary of RTCA SC-159 GPS Integrity Working Group Activities,"," *Navigation, Journal of the Institute of Navigation* 44(4):499-500, Winter 1997-1998.
86. Farrell, J.L., "Unfinished Business: Glaring Absences from the Achievement List," in *PLANS 2004, Position Location and Navigation Symposium*, IEEE Cat. No. 04CH37556, 573-580, IEEE - Institute of Electrical and Electronics Engineers, Monterey, CA, April 26-29, 2004. https://doi.org/10.1109/PLANS.2004.1309044.
87. Nisner, P.D. and Johannessen, R., "Ten Million Data Points from TSO-Approved Aviation GPS Receivers: Results of Analysis and Applications to Design and Use in Aviation," *Navigation, Journal of the Institute of Navigation* 47(1):43-50, 2000. https://doi.org/10.1002/j.2161-4296.2000.tb02421.x.
88. Farrell, J.L., "Kalman Filter, Strapdown, Imaging, Tracking, and More," James L Farrell, August 25, 2010,

https://jameslfarrell.com/kalman-filter-strapdown-imaging-tracking-and-more/, accessed April 7, 2020.

89. Farrell, J.L., "Simulation of a Minimum Variance Orbital Navigation System," in *Proceedings of AIAA 3rd Manned Space Flight Meeting*, Houston, TX, November 1964, https://doi.org/10.2514/6.1964-1206, also in *AIAA Journal of Spacecraft and Rockets* 44(1):91-98, January 1966.
90. Morton, J., Parkinson, B.W., Spilker, J.J., and van Diggelen, F. (Eds.), Gao, G., and Lo, S. (Assoc. Eds.), *Position Navigation & Timing technologies in the 21st Century* (Hoboken, NJ: Wiley-IEEE, 2020).
91. Farrell, J.L., "Kalman Filtering: Still More Work to be Done," in *Proceedings of the 30th International Technical Meeting of the Satellite Division of The Institute of Navigation (ION GNSS+ 2017)*, Portland, OR, September 2017, 1790-1799, https://doi.org/10.33012/2017.15191.
92. Farrell, James L., "Book on Tracking," James L Farrell, March 5, 2011, https://jameslfarrell.com/book-on-tracking, accessed April 7, 2020.
93. Farrell, J.L. and van Graas, F.. "Containment Limits for Free-Inertial Coast," in *Proceedings of the 23rd International Technical Meeting of the Satellite Division of The Institute of Navigation (ION GNSS 2010)*, Portland, OR, 2010, 1490-1497, https://jameslfarrell.com/wp-content/uploads/2013/08/GNSS2010.pdf.
94. Farrell, J.L., "Panel question submitted by James L. Farrell," in *Proceedings of the 13th International Technical Meeting of the Satellite Division of The Institute of Navigation (ION GPS 2000)*, Salt Lake City, UT, September 2000, 1420.

Contact Information

EDGEresearch@sae.org

The authors of this document together with the SAE Team responsible for its creation join in expressing our deepest appreciation to all of the individuals who contributed.

www.ingramcontent.com/pod-product-compliance
Lightning Source LLC
LaVergne TN
LVHW070912210926
848482LV00017B/1057
9781468601787